Still A Solider

LC Johnson

with

Beth Volpert Johansen

FIRST EDITION

Copyright © 2017 LC Johnson, Beth Volpert Johansen

Cover Art, Joe Voisin

All rights reserved.

LC Johnson, Publisher

Library of Congress Cataloging-in-publication data applied for.

ISBN-13: 978-0692893623 (LC Johnson)

ISBN-10: 0692893628

For my family, friends, and all those with whom I have enjoyed countless meaningful conversations. Thank you and may God bless each of you for your influence in my life.

-LC

Thank you to my family, friends, and readers for all of your support, advice, edits, readings and prayers during this journey. I am also grateful to Randy Wayne White for advising me to write relentlessly.

-Beth

Still a Soldier

Table of Contents

*MVT: Most Valuable Tool

Acknowledgements

This memoir is actually a salute to all of you out there in this wide world who have had an influence on my life. Of course, there are too many people to name individually. I would leave names out and that just wouldn't do at all. Besides, I am sure I will meet someone new today and tomorrow and the next day.

I greatly appreciate all of the places I frequent for their hospitality and greetings each day, especially Magnolia Bakery where many planning meetings and interviews took place.

Each of the board members I have served with over the years has had a lasting impact on my life. Those in the military and education arenas who learned lessons right beside me will always have my respect and admiration. All of the churches I have attended over my 80 plus years have certainly helped me to keep my moral compass pointed in the right direction. Of course, my family, beginning with my parents for raising me right, has been the biggest influence and I am grateful for their love.

Thank you to NightGlass Media Group for all of your help, patience, and advice and for the loan of my coauthor. This has been a real adventure and we appreciate your guidance.

I do want to mention that I am especially grateful to all those who shared their conversations with us for the publication of this book.
LC

Introduction

A good name is to be chosen rather than great riches, and favor is better than silver or gold.
Proverbs 22:1

My name is LC Johnson. It is a pretty simple name. By way of introduction, it works just fine. As a kid, the people who called my name did so with more respect than anyone would anticipate for a little black kid in southern Mississippi.

While I was in the military, my name was associated with the virtues my family expected of me; trustworthiness, hard work, and dependability with a healthy dash of ingenuity. During my tenure in the education field, my name brought with it a sense of accomplishment and always leaving a place better than when I found it. Introducing myself has always been the key to starting conversations with people. Upon retirement, I found that I had a few more crucial introductions and conversations left in me.

In my estimation, I have had four distinct "tours of duty" in my lifetime. My "tours" began on the home front in Mississippi, extended throughout our world during my time in the United States Air Force, and brought me to the fighting front of educational challenges. I would like to think this last "tour" as a servant for civic and social activity will suit me until I am promoted to heaven.

When my wife, Gracie, and I looked for somewhere to retire, I reached out to my real estate agent from New York to ask her for a recommendation in the Atlanta area. With my mother being in a care facility in Jackson, MS, I needed to be in a central transportation hub in case I needed to reach her in a hurry. Atlanta seemed to offer a new challenge as well. The criteria I asked for included a neighborhood with great schools.

Norcross High School and the area around it appeared to have good schools, active churches, and an involved civic life. I figured I would check into a few things; get in involved at church, maybe even volunteer at the school. As you might have guessed, I did volunteer once or twice and now I enjoy a seat on a variety of boards helping to make decisions about my neighborhood and the surrounding county of Gwinnett. I was even able to spend some quality time with my new neighbors forming a city out of our slice of unincorporated Gwinnett.

It makes Gracie, and I very proud to be able to say we live in Peachtree Corners. It is from here, from my second floor office that my pup, Oscar, and I make some big and some little decisions that help guide our county. By way of getting involved in my community…again, certain patterns and tools born of thousands of conversations began to play around in my mind's eye. It began to seem important that I share the thoughts, ideas and my (hopefully) humble opinions of how I see our world today. I hope that the reader of this book finds some value in my musings that have taken the form of a memoir-biography-self-help publication.

Where I have landed, here in Gwinnett County, Georgia seems to mirror the world in which I have lived my life. We have people here from many walks of life, from different countries speaking languages other than English who want to find their place in a county that is a real melting pot. I find myself among the powers that be as a sort of bridge to the collection of minority communities that make their homes here.

My job, not that anyone is actually my employer, is to help connect these people to one another in a way that suits everyone. To do that, I use the lessons learned during my youth in the Deep South, my service to my country, my tenure as an educator, and my time serving on a variety of boards all over the world.

Chapter 1
Conversations...How I get things done

Conversations with love...Romans 9:2-21

"Start a conversation; just start a conversation wherever you are...talk about anything...just start the conversation and get to know people." LC Johnson

Growing up on a cotton farm in southern Mississippi might have provided me with a somewhat narrow view of the world. I have to give credit to the people in my life for helping me see past the rural nature of cotton farming as a means to make a living and help me to see there might be something else I could do with my life. I spent a great deal of time in the company of my elders. Funny to think, now I am an elder. I guess that gives me some edge, but I still think of myself as a lifelong learner, not always a teacher. As a kid, I watched and listened. You had to listen and not be heard, that was common knowledge. It was also common sense if you didn't want to get taken down a notch or two. Watching and listening helped create a sense of respect for the opinions of those with more years on this earth than I had at the time. That is something, I fear, we lack these days. Not to say kids are not smart and can't have their own ideas. It's just that it seems to me, a healthy respect for elders is in decline.

The conversations that older people had, the wisdom that came from them was probably lost on me. At least I didn't think it all that valuable at the time. Later, as I thought about spending my future in Flora, I began to listen to what those folks had to say. I can't say I took all of the advice, but I did think about it all. Those conversations taught me to listen well to other people. If I started a conversation with someone and really listened to what they had to tell me, then I learned about what they needed or wanted and what they were all about. When I learned what people were about, I could work them into what I might need at the time by providing something of value to them. You see, you have to help someone see a reason for helping you accomplish something. That way, they feel they got some value for themselves by helping someone else.

Air Force Conversations

Joining the military provided plenty of fuel for great conversations that I used to move my career along. It wasn't all self-serving, but I did take the best bits of this and that to fill the needs other people had. The most effective conversations were not necessarily with those in the highest command. Not to say that I didn't hold them in great esteem, but they were not always approachable in a conversational manner. Making the all-important introduction started the most productive conversations I had and then, by using a few well-placed questions, most people would just start talking. I listened carefully. I took note of the places in their stories where I thought I might be able to use their information to make my tour of duty more beneficial to us both...or for an entire platoon for that matter.

School System Conversations

One of the things I got pretty good at was starting conversations with people who could help us bring significant change to the schools I was working in. From the time I began my career with youth in the detention system to working alongside Rudy Crew, conversations never failed to help me take things out of my toolbox or add new tools. When I stepped foot onto the campus of Luther Burbank High School in Sacramento, it never occurred to me that I would add so many more tools to my box. The way I had it figured, I had enough tools in my box to tackle the huge problems facing that school. Little did I know, the students, families and surrounding community would cause me to shake up my neatly arranged toolbox.

I learned a lot from all of them-mostly by starting a conversation and then again, listening carefully to the pieces of their story. The conversations that eventually made a huge difference to the educational arenas in which I taught and counseled were sort of like filling in pieces to a puzzle. I got bits here and there; from the community, families, teachers, staff, and, administration that helped complete the puzzle. But the most important idea exchanges I had during my time in education were with the students themselves. Helping them discover the answers to all of the challenges they faced sharpened my skill set and I began to use the tools I already had in a much more effective way.

Civic and Social Duty Conversations

Now, I like to say I got out of the business of business, education, and the military so I could retire. Retirement just did not turn out to be what I thought it was going to look like. When Gracie and I retired, we had a wonderful home in a vibrant county, an active church, and plenty to keep us occupied. I guess the desire to serve and share the best of the tools I had collected over the years just overcame any joy that I could possibly get from sitting on the couch watching game shows and baseball.

So I started a conversation. And another. And yet, another. One thing led to another and, before I could blink, there I was...involved again. You have to be careful with conversations, you can end up doing more than you ever anticipated and finding that you like it that way. I have this huge office overlooking our neighborhood. It is filled with books by people who know some things. The walls and shelves house hundreds of little, and some not-so-little awards reminding me of a very busy and influential and influenced life. As I sat in my freshly decorated office, it occurred to me I might want to step outside for a while, walk my dog, Oscar, talk to some people, get to know my neighbors, join a group or two, invite someone to coffee. That's how it starts folks; having a conversation.

MVT: If you want to connect with someone, just start a conversation. Find out where they are coming from, where they want to go, what you might learn from each other.

Chapter 2
Building Up The Toolbox...tools of my trade

So the craftsman encourages the smelter, And he who smooths metal with the hammer encourages him who beats the anvil, Saying of the soldering, "It is good"; And he fastens it with nails, So that it will not totter. Isaiah 41:7

Conversational Tools

Like I said, having a conversation begins with an introduction. Simple, plain, honest, earnest introductions are easy, yet priceless. If you listen carefully and have enough conversations, you begin to connect people, events, needs, wants, social movements, and a whole host of governmental necessities. Having people who are skilled at making these connections is crucial to the success of any entity.

Be it government, charity, education, business-all these areas are connected in some way or another. Holding a conversation with a bank president at Rotary might lead to fulfilling a need that the Salvation Army may have. I am part of both of those groups which gives me a certain perspective when holding a conversation. I can see both sides and maybe pair them up. You see how that works? It's important stuff, these conversations. They keep the cogs turning.

Tools from my Home Front

I learned early on that I didn't really want to be a farmer in southern Mississippi in the 1950's and 1960's or beyond. Our farm in Flora, MS was productive. It was where I learned lots of things young men need to know before they go out into the world. I learned about screwdrivers, hammers, saws, and wrenches. Knowing how to fix things as they broke down was a necessity on a farm. Cotton didn't grow itself and finding a way to keep farmhands who were considerably older than me in line and on the job meant watching my elders, learning their ways, and developing communication tools that did not alienate our employees while keeping my status as employer in tact.

Because I was very young when I began driving a car and working a cotton farm, I had to walk a fine line with plenty of confidence, but avoid coming off cocky or, as they would say back then, "too big for his britches." Eventually, I would add some very valuable tools to my toolbox. Each one of those tools was honed to a reasonable sharpness by the lessons I took away from my hometown.

Tools from the Military

My time in the Air Force helped me to visualize a toolbox that I began to fill with great advice, common sense, habits, ethics, and a variety of stuff that would come in very handy at any given time. Collecting tools became a subconscious thing for me. I guess I sort of weeded out the things that made sense to keep or try out and threw out the things that just didn't seem to fit. The military taught me how to work the system without calling attention to myself in a negative manner. It was not long before I realized that saving time was a valuable tool. If I could save anyone time, from the lowest ranking airman to those in full charge of the base, then I was considered valuable myself and it showed in all of my performance reviews.

Tools from Public Education

Filling that toolbox through conversations is what laid the groundwork for my future in management. Though "management" is a really broad term, the places those tools would take me prepared me to write my dissertation in managing people to do really good work. Listening, talking through ideas, and facilitating goals you are attempting to achieve-that is why people meet formally.

So many times during meetings, I found that people talked over each other and you don't get the main ingredients for what you need to accomplish goals if participants are talking over each other. The talkers talk louder and so many great ideas get silenced because more timid members are not willing to interrupt the squeaky wheels-so to speak. To be a good leader, to facilitate an effective meeting, you have to politely control the need for some folks to have to be heard above others or you won't get anything done. Working that out, working out the way a meeting should run ended up being one of the most valuable tools in my box. During my time in education, my toolbox shaped up to be a guide for me in all that I would eventually become involved with on boards of directors and in administration. But, that's getting ahead of myself here.

Tools from Active Civic and Public Service

Sometimes, you have to facilitate a conversation between two or more people who represent a world of cultures, economic status, and personalities. Face it, we all look very different from one another. Despite the fact that I am a very dark man, I see no reason to be uncomfortable meeting new people of any race or culture. In fact, I kind of thrive on it. But not everyone sees opportunity in a room full of people who have a world of differences attached to their coat tails floating in behind them. I see the possibilities arising from what each could learn from the other if they would just introduce themselves. Some might, some hesitate, and some never will. I guess that is where my "status" as an elder comes in handy. I can get away with pairing up two people and opening up a dialogue that needs opened; no matter how "edgy" the topics might be (as the kids are fond of saying these days).

Management Tools

I want to take a minute to mention a few thoughts on management. It is the subject of much of my higher education and I have found that it varies just a little from situation to situation. Management is management and if you use common sense and visibility and communicate with people. You can manage people. You have to have expectations of them and they need to have expectations of you. I think that is the most important piece of dealing with people. There's personality coming from both sides. There will always be disagreement, but you sit down and discuss the disagreement. And that's what management is about. We need more of that today across the board.

Applying the tools

This toolbox I built over my 80+ years is certainly something of my own imagination. I can see myself in each "tour" of my life carefully collecting tools, honing them, and making them a part of my personality. The value of each tool, has served me well over the years.

The one constant and concrete tool in my imaginary box was, is, and always will be my bible. There are lessons there that began as stories bouncing off my juvenile brain until they slowly began to sink in and produce new meaning for me. It might seem trivial to distill each chapter into a verse, but a reader has to have something tangible to hang on to when considering the intangible nature of the tools I have gathered over the years.

MVT: Keep a mental toolbox of what works and what does not work. It will serve you well.

Chapter 3
The Home Front...Influential Flora, a solid base and my first tools

"Train a Child in the way he should go, even when he is old, he will not depart." Proverbs 22:6

It is funny how one or two conversations with the right person can send you on a completely different path. It was kind of like putting a few things in a toolbox to use later on. The people of Flora provided me with a moral compass that was the first, and I think, most important tool I ever placed I that box.

I was born and raised in rural Flora, Mississippi, the only son of middle-class farmers, Matilda and Lee Johnson. We had more than most around us. We had a television, plenty of food, and a nice home on 50 acres. According to those in the community, I was thought to be a respectful and respected young man who understood the economics and science of cotton growing, processing, and sales better than most his age.

I have to credit any maturity and ability to visualize the bigger picture with the way I was raised. I used to hang out around older men; they used to sit around and talk about their lives-positive stuff, not negative stuff. So, I grew up with more than two hands, a variety of other people that was instrumental in maintaining my morals and what-have-you.

My upbringing included a deeply enriching church life. It was there, at the church, that we attended social activities that were conducive to our lifestyle. On Sunday's the family attended church anywhere from 1-3 times a day- morning, afternoon and evening. It wasn't too difficult, because, you see, the farm sort of surrounded the church grounds there and so we sort of blended in and out all day long.

All the things I was taught during my upbringing was always positive. It was demanded that I stay away from bad things. A lot of encouragement came from older men. They were sort of like an extended family, so I had a lot of interaction with older people.

Growing up in the South, the opportunity did not present itself to learn the real world. But also, growing up in the South and being a farmer, I had an opportunity to interact with some of the white farmers and I picked up quite a bit of knowledge in how you facilitate selling your products to the buyers.

There were three gins in the Flora area that were owned by three different people. So, interacting with those people, I learned how to market the cotton sales. I learned a great deal through that process. Now, I was able to find out who was paying the most for cotton through interaction with those people and other people around them. Their "riders" or whatever you wanted to call them at that time, knew who was going to get the best deal. And since I knew them, I would hear, "Mr. So-And-So is paying more than Mr. So-And-So".

I attended the segregated Burgess High School, in Flora, MS. It was named for the principal, Mr. R.W. Burgess. The civic and social activism climates were heating up during my attendance there. In fact, our principal, Mr.

Burgess had joined the NAACP early on and felt some of that heat. It was strongly suggested to him that he resign.

Even though Flora was not an openly racist town, well, you could understand what they meant and he did resign. His family moved to California, but I lost contact with them. It did make me think though.

What really motivated me to move into the military arena - if you will- is this young man who had grown up in the same area that I lived in. He had gone into the Air Force. This young man who was older than I...he was probably 4-5 years older than I was at the time and he came back on his leave - what they call leave- for about 30 days, so I got a chance to see this young person and this blue jacket really intrigued me and I thought, I would really love to have that jacket. I think it was called a B-15 jacket. It just stood out so well. I said I would like to have one of those jackets one day.

I don't recall having too much give and take in any conversations I had in Flora growing up, I mostly listened. It was one particular conversation I had with my math teacher Mr. McMillan that really set things up for me to find my way to greater things and get a few steps closer to the world represented by that blue jacket. Mr. McMillan, who was also a minister, lived in a place called Canton, MS. He had been in WW II. And he suggested to me all the things that were evolving around me was not the best thing for me....all the stuff going on in the South particularly, and he suggested to me that I should get the heck out of Flora, MS and broaden my knowledge of what's going on in the world. He told me, "I would encourage you to choose an opportunity to maybe go into the military and I would also encourage you to also consider going into the Air Force. It's more challenging and you would probably stay away from combat and all those wonderful things." How far off that he was…but I will always be thankful to Mr. McMillan for suggesting I get out.

So I ended up going in the Air Force based on seeing this young man that had been part of the military and this "authority figure" man enforcing that I should consider another option for my life. Joining the military didn't exactly fit my reputation because, at the time, we were farmers - my mom and dad and I were farmers. My dad and his father were fortunate enough back in the 1950's to own their own land and farm. Together, we would farm that land and have people come in and work the farm for us; along with us.

That was another reason that I wanted to get an opportunity to move on. My father had suggested to me, since we owned this land of 50 acres, that "we" can (you can) do the farming. He determined it would be a good thing for himself to go off and participate in this thing called public working where people could go work outside of the farm, outside of the home. He planned on doing just that while turning the farm over to my mom and me. He thought it might look enticing to me, since I had such a wonderful reputation with the merchants and the owners of large spreads, to rent some of that land and have people come in to where I could just kind of supervise… Back then, they didn't know the words "yeah, that's right". So I'm sayin' underneath my breath, "yeah, that's right". The next thing they knew, I had been to Jackson, which is the embarkation for people that's going into the military.

I went on a Friday. I think I caught the bus from Flora to Jackson. I went through and took all the tests that you had to take. And the next thing I knew, I was on my way to Lackland AFB in Texas with some knowledge about how things worked in the South to put in my personal toolbox for use at a later time. Knowing I had no intention to ever attend college, most of the town, both black and white, figured I would follow in my father's footsteps, get married, work the farm, and live the rural Mississippi life. I pretty much had it figured differently. My "place" in Flora society was one of respect for the hard work I provided on the family farm, my love of God, and in the trust placed in me by local, white cotton gin owners for my ability to organize local young men for the loading and unloading of cotton from the gins to the boxcars.

When the cotton gin owners asked my dad where "his boy" was, Lee Johnson told them his "boy" had gone to San Antonio, TX to join the Air Force. My dad later told me that all that one owner could do was shake his head and say, "Well, I'll be damned."

Despite the fact that I had left my birthplace in Flora, I still didn't forget my mom and dad. Each month, I sent funds directly to them from my pay. With the support I was able to provide, they were able to move to Jackson, Mississippi where they bought a nice home in a pleasant neighborhood where they did all the things people are supposed to do. Their street was filled with middle class people that looked just like them. They had garden clubs and dinners and the like. It was a nice existence only it was all African American.

Segregation was firmly entrenched for them. Their home was just a few blocks from the Medgar Evars home, where he was eventually shot for his role in the fight for civil rights. With that kind of proximity to those interested in furthering civil rights, my parents were witnesses to how things looked from the South.

From where I stood in the Air Force, my witness and experience was somewhat different. We had military personnel of all colors, only we were not promoted the same. I would eventually see some of that change during my service, but on the home front, very little changed. It was an observation that eventually bolstered the lessons I had learned from the older gentlemen I kept company with. Listening was a most valuable tool and it would serve me well throughout my own life using my own methods for changing the status quo, so-to-speak.

MVT: Listen to your elders, build your circle of influence and become trusted. This will establish your moral compass.

Chapter 4
Military Duty Tour of Duty…the United States Air Force
Lackland AFB, Japan, Korea, Vietnam, Thailand, Europe, California…

"Whom shall I send, who will go for us?" Isaiah 6:8

"Do not be frightened, and do not be dismayed, for the Lord your God is with you wherever you go." Joshua 1:9

As with any military career, I started with basic training in March of 1954. For a young man straight out of Southern Mississippi, basic training dished up several lessons in reality. Of course, I received training for my place in the Air Force; that was expected. Service in the military would end up rewarding me with so much more. Additionally, life outside of Flora also served to show me that the circumstances my math teacher had alluded to with regard to growing civil rights unrest were very real.

My basic training at Lackland Air Force Base in Texas was the beginning of my journey through adult life. There was so much to learn, so many decisions to make, so many people to talk to. More importantly, there were so many people I found I should listen to. Listening turned out to be one of my most powerful tools. Putting my own talk in check so that I could really hear what people were saying became one of the most useful things I learned. It really was the most basic of my training and left me with a platform for lifelong learning.

First Stop...the not-so-settled West

From basic training I was assigned to the remote Continental Divide Air Force Station in New Mexico. It was a radar site west of Thoreau, New Mexico back when the Cold War was really at the height of activity. Because it was a small place in New Mexico where there were no African Americans or blacks much at all at that time, I didn't exactly receive a warm reception. As it happened, I had to be sent to another station, which was in Moriarty, New Mexico. Moriarty, well, that was, er, shall we say, a little more...diverse. Enough about that.

Moriarty seemed to be a good deal more relaxed about people of color. There were about 200 people on the radar site. As a result of being so close-knit and family-like, I got to meet the sergeants and the officers. My job was mostly counting nuts and bolts to facilitate the radar systems. I did my job, excelled where I could, and tried very hard to make myself more than useful.

The time there, doing a simple job, but doing it as well as I could, led me to start thinking of ways to do it better. It was a time of innovation on many fronts, and my little boxes of nuts and bolts was one small front where I could do the simplest job in the most efficient manner. It got me noticed which only began to help my career and steer me towards larger, more involved fronts, so-to-speak. From Moriarty, in June of 1955, I transferred out to Kirtland AFB on my way to Parks AFB in preparation for transport to the Far East.

Japan, 1955...Welcome to the wider world son

Now, you have to understand something here. New Mexico wasn't all that foreign. It certainly wasn't Mississippi, but, for the most part, it was just another state in the US of A. My transport and subsequent time in Japan, well, that was something altogether different.

First off, a fishing boat on a lake does not qualify anyone to determine personal seaworthiness. I can honestly say that I didn't see much of anything aboard the USS A.E. Anderson except my bunk and the latrine for the entire trip from California to Japan. There was not much about the chow that appealed to me either. Saltines acted as the four major food groups for the duration. Being an airman kind of gave the hope that transport might be of the winged variety, but sea legs were required for many a trip over the course of my military career.

My destination was Tachikawa, Japan and I was never so happy to see dry land. Tachikawa, that's where things really began to blossom for me.

Cook Much? Nope

I guess stereotypes are all in how you look at them. Getting upset and angry might make a statement, but I don't believe it to be productive. Somehow, it is kind of like taking a knee during the National Anthem. It's just not called for. I know my parents wouldn't have put up with that kind of behavior. So, when certain assumptions were made about a young man of color from Mississippi likely being a good candidate for providing meals to his counterparts, it didn't take anger to point out the errors in their thinking. I just had to cook once or twice. Turns out, I was far better at supplying the food than I was at preparing it.

Through a few well-timed conversations, I managed to make my point with the Mess Sergeant, as he was called. On the weekends, I would volunteer my time to work over at the mess hall. I learned how to wash the dishes and I learned how to clean the grease trap.

Seemed my kitchen tools were so poor that a Classification Action Request was initiated by my CO to remove me from the 374th Food Service Squadron to the 374th Air Base Group. The report cited, "... it became very evident that he was not adapt (adept) nor particularly interested in becoming a cook...". I can't really report that my feelings were hurt. That request got me out of the kitchen in short order.

In addition to my lousy food prep skills, a few good conversations with the man in charge pushed my cause just enough to further my career in the right direction. You see, after talking with me, the sergeant discovered there was a great deal to the "boy" from the South. He took a liking to me and he told me I needed something better than the mess, so he made sure to look up my entry test scores. He offered me some tutoring to bring my test scores up and then he looked to send me on to do something more productive within the organization. That's how I really began to catch on to what it would take to move on up. I added a few tool adjustments to the conversational tools I already had in my box while I had his expertise at my disposal.

From the kitchen, I headed into supply chain work. There was this one supervisor I had that I will never forget. He was a great guy-red-headed guy from somewhere up north. But, he had a friend who ran the NCO club, the officer's club, and the airmen's club. He got me a job at the airman's club as the night manager. I would count the money, stock the bar and all that sort of stuff. Figuring out how to handle money became one very important tool in my box that would continue to serve me well over the years.

In all, I spent 2 years in Japan at Tachikawa AFB, where I made lots of friends. Watching out for the money and supplies made me visible as a reliable guy who understood the importance of accountability in inventory and finances. All this was a good thing because when I had first arrived in Japan, the powers that be had me pegged for kitchen duty and I needed a quick way out of that mess-so to speak.

It might be interesting note that during my time in Japan I was to be awarded my first Good Conduct Medal for Efficiency, Honor, and Fidelity which was a source of pride and spurred me on to continue on my path that would soon include furthering my education. It was in September of 1956 that I was promoted from Airman 3rd Class to Airman 2nd Class.

Stateside Again

I returned to the States, THE US of A, in June 1957 and was very happy to be on American soil. On 30 June 1957 I reported to Lincoln AFB in Nebraska with the 818th Air Base Group. I have to tell you, Lincoln was a strategic air command base out in the boonies. I worked in something they called pre-issue. This is where they would repair the assets on the aircraft if there was any kind of deficiency. They would bring it into the repair shop where my job began. I had to be responsible for keeping track of it. It was a challenge to keep a good log of what aircraft it came off and where it would go back.

Lincoln was also the place where my quest for extending my formal education began to take root. I began to realize that education, formal education, had a certain value beyond what I thought I knew coming out of Flora. My formal education began with training classes in security measures that gave me clearance to certain documents. The Cold War played a huge part in the increase in secrecy and we had all manner of documents to sign swearing allegiance and promising never to divulge classified information. The Cold War made folks pretty paranoid, I think.

I was at Lincoln for about a year. Important people noticed my work, made comments along the way and recommended me as a problem-solver. So, here again, interacting with different people from different backgrounds, I was able to add to the toolbox that I brought in with me from my parents' teaching as well as the lessons I learned in Japan about managing supplies.

That's how I began to impress people above me. I was hoping they were thinking, "This guy has some reliability, some integrity, so we are going to make sure we kind of monitor him- we are going to continue to do things to continue to build his toolbox to become a very successful military person." At least that is how they treated me. In any case it was all a world of difference from life in Flora, MS and that, in my opinion, was a very good thing.

To Reenlist? That was a good question

Things were going pretty well for me in the Air Force, so when it came time, I reenlisted. There was some hesitation because I had not realized any movement from Airman Second Class, but I figured with the racially charged climate, the Air Force was as good a place as any to work. Besides, I was already well-invested in my higher education which was essentially free. That, in itself, was a pay raise. The value of an education was beginning to become very clear to me in those early days.

On 9 May 1958, I reported to March AFB in Riverside, CA. This was far different than anywhere else I had lived to this time and I felt pretty fortunate to spend about four years in California at March. I kept a small article from a newspaper. It's all yellowed now, but at the time, it made March AFB sound pretty good. The paper called it, "A city within itself."

According to my records, I joined the 320th Air Maintenance Squadron which was associated with the 320th Bombardment Wing Medium. The real significance here is that we were under the Air Expeditionary Deterrent Force designed to deter Cold War issues. I guess, with all the racial tensions back home in The South, the Cold War brewing up trouble in the forefront, and Elvis Presley joining the Army, my reenlistment wasn't big news to much of anyone, but I thought it to be a really big deal given my other choice was still, well...cotton.

I'll be the first to admit, the California sunshine kind of sank into my bones where the memory of it was to stay put even during four long years in the English countryside. But, we are getting ahead of the story.

At March AFB, I worked in the supply tool issue and pre-issue department of the supply chain. I had some very good supervisors and very good mentors. They knew that I had begun to catch on to a lot of stuff. I did not go out of the purview of what I was supposed to be doing. I was very prompt in my being at work and being on time. And doing my job in an outstanding manner. That was a word they used throughout the military: Outstanding-Poor-Needs Extra Help...A source of deep satisfaction for me came with each evaluation I received and the pressure applied by my supervisors to help me find a promotion was in some way or another always included on those reports. It helped me swallow the frustration at watching other men, good men, but predominantly white men find promotions well ahead of me. It taught me great patience and that, in itself, was one of the most important tools I would ever lay in my personal toolbox.

Tool Crib...if it's broke; then fix it

The funny thing was, while I was gathering these intrinsic tools for a toolbox of my imagination, I could have had no idea that real tools and toolboxes would come to have a huge influence on my progression "up the ranks". The military had some ideas about how things should be run. By using the intrinsic tools I had collected along the way by means of experience, I was able to make improvements upon the "tool cribs" used by those who supplied and maintained anything and everything with an engine. For this, I received some good recognition that, eventually, led to a promotion in February of 1961 from A2C to A1C.

My first really big "Tool Crib Challenge" took place in May of 1961 while I was still at March AFB in California. My group was charged with relocating an entire A&E (Armaments & Electronics) Tool Crib. This is where specialized equipment is stored for testing on highly secret and classified equipment related to the flying mission. The many hours that I put into the job and the attention to detail landed me in charge of the whole shebang! From there, it was recommended that I be sent to NCO Preparatory School which fit in nicely with my conscious decision to further my education.

My Tech Sgt, Nolan Renfroe said, "He will reap a great deal of personal satisfaction by improving himself educationally, not only will this be most expedient to him in his service career, but of great value when he is returned to civilian life." Truer words were never written as far as I am concerned.

TSgt Renfroe also noted in one of my evaluations that I was pretty good at finding lost "stuff". The military has a lot of "stuff" and keeping all of it inventoried is a particularly daunting challenge. I completed assemblies, ordered components to complete ill-used equipment that was just laying around waiting to be repaired, and gained control over the tools and equipment by improving the record keeping efforts in the crib.

One of the other things that I was good at was filling a need and profiting from it in my spare time. I was a 2-striper at the time, but I was sort of a leader from within the squadron. People kind of looked up to me. And also, there was a 1st Sergeant - I think he had been an engineer on a B-36 and he really looked out for me when it came to opportunity. On holidays, I would take the shifts for people that did not want to pull their CQ or KP. For me, it was a business. I did have a slight disadvantage in that I was still not always respected due to color, but he made sure - this was when you had to go through and salute to get paid- that those people that owed me money paid up.

Lakenheath RAF...welcome to England

Well now, this was about as far removed from life in Flora as I had ever been exposed to. Accents are accents, but you couldn't get too much different from a deep southern twang than Lakenheath and still be speaking English. And the food, well, it was different.

It was 1962 and civil rights in America were roaring loudly. England was a nice respite that allowed me to continue furthering my own career and send money home to my parents because I had virtually no personal overhead costs. Each month, I sent funds directly to them from my pay. With the support I was able to provide, they were able to move to Jackson, Mississippi where they bought a nice home in a pleasant neighborhood where they did all the things people are supposed to do. Their street was filled with middle class people that looked just like them. They had garden clubs and dinners and the like. It was a nice existence, only, it was an all African-American existence; everyone insulated from one another.

Segregation was firmly entrenched for them. From where I stood, we had military personnel of all colors, only we were not promoted the same. I would eventually see some of that change during my service, but on the home front, very little changed.

I served under USAFE (United States Air Force in Europe) while I was stationed in England. It was there that I took as many training courses as possible, which taught me more about supply chain and tool crib operations. Whether I chose to continue on in service or head for civilian life, these classes were an outstanding tool for my box that could be used in the management of things or people.

Now, the military uses some pretty interesting terminology, much of which ended up under my purview. "Welfare Fund Property" turned out to be code for "Gymnasium Equipment." It was an additional duty tacked onto my Command Equipment Management Team work. Seems the more you did, the more they gave you to do. But, because of all the "extras" I was again named Squadron Airman of the Month twice over. I found in England, the quality of my "dress" was every bit as important as the quality of my work, which, according to the records was, "highly efficient". Additionally, the powers that be were beginning to catch on to my ability to memorize Allowance and Authorization Procedures along with parts numbers and manual passages. Memorization was a key tool in my box that I would pull out time and again over the years long after my return to civilian life.

I was selected as my Squadron's Airman of the Month based on my abilities, along with my correct and courteous military bearing. It also didn't hurt that no matter where I went, money was saved. That kind of became my "thing" and it wasn't long before my TSgt, Patrick J. McBreen took note. He was a ruddy sort of fella who represented all things "British" to me. The one marked difference between he and his American counterparts is that he never, ever seemed to notice I was any different than any other Airman. I even received the personal attention of Major Earl Le Duc, USAF 48th Tactical who said of me, "His professional approach to complicated authorization problems compares favorably with performance of senior NCO's." The good Major personally recommended my immediate promotion.

Despite being awarded Airman of the Month for my Squadron more than once, a Good Conduct Medal and Air Force Outstanding Unit Award in 1964, and The Air Force Commendation Medal for meritorious service through 1965, it would be another year before I saw my actual promotion from A1C to Staff Sergeant. While I did eventually find recognition for my skills, the pervasive idea that somehow, because I was black, my work wasn't significant enough to warrant promotion for several years. Airman First Class uniform insignias became worn before they could be replaced by way of a change in rank.

Through the first ten years of my service, I gained more and more responsibility as my superior officers recognized my abilities, but that didn't result in rapid promotions. Overwhelmingly, my superior officers wrote time and again on my behalf recommending promotion. Those were different times during which the rules varied greatly depending upon the color of your skin. Instead of wallowing in some sort of counterproductive self-pity, I just kept on making myself useful with my ear turned towards the conversations going on around me all the while gathering new tools that would come in handy in the future.

Stateside Again...Laredo, TX and that long-awaited promotion

Back in the saddle again! At least that is how it felt to be back in the warm, sunny south once again. I wondered if maybe I was a little too courteous, well mannered, and well dressed for Laredo since having just come in from the proper English countryside. In any case, I was happy to be home. Plus, the food, I had really missed "American" food.

At Laredo, I continued to improve my efficiency ratings in the areas of supply. For me, it was a little personal to improve a little each evaluation. With an error rate of less than 2% on my monthly transactions, it was a real challenge to make improvements, but it gave me something to focus my frustrations on.

The absolutely most significant event during my time at Laredo would be realizing the movement from Airman to Sergeant on 1 February 1966. This was five long years of work finally rewarded since I had first been made an Airman 1st Class. It was a great feeling that coincided with a 100% due-out reconciliation rating on my evaluation. I was certainly looking for perfection and I managed it. I guess the US Air Force just couldn't argue with THAT!

Korea...1967

Korea was a place of most significant personal change for me. Growing up in the Deep South, I had thought I had seen hunger, abuses, mistreatments, and suffering. Perspective is a humbling experience and until now, I had been riding the wave of my own accomplishments not fully understanding humility. To say I was truly humbled is an understatement.

My tour in Korea was extended due to the capture of the Pueblo in January of 1968. This was when my personal toolbox really started to fill-because, we're talking Korea now, it was sort of a real "Best Kept Secret" in the Air Force to go to Korea because there were not a lot of things going on over there. We were sort of keepers of the island, more-or-less. Then the boat incident occurred and things went all to hell. My point is, I was an NCO and during the Kennedy era, African Americans or people of color were not being promoted stripe-wise or whatever-wise and that came out. They put a system in place, and they made it mandatory.

There, in Korea, I was a part of the officers. I was with the big guys who sat around to try to plan how, if we were attacked, how we were going to facilitate our safety. I was part of making those kinds of decisions. An enlisted person; sitting with the colonel, the majors and the captains and lieutenants. So, my bucket - my toolbox was really growing from there in ways I had never expected.

It was at Osan AFB that I would be able to use my toolbox to save my government more than 1.2 million dollars. It was also at Osan AFB, in our spare time, that some of my fellow Airmen and I would spend time in the company of the children doing little more than surviving day-to-day at an orphanage. I had experienced some of that growing up.

We taught lessons in English to the children, but what was most remarkable was their hunger for human interaction. It made me think, for the first time, about the power of speaking to another human being. It also made me realize that I would not get along in life on the education I had pursued thus far. Seeing injustices happening to our fellow human beings when they were not educated to find a way up and out was heartbreaking.

I vowed to not only pursue education for myself, but I think it may have spurred me to realize that I might want to share education with others one day.

Korea was the birth of my passion to "just begin a conversation" with people of all shapes, sizes, ethnicities, education levels, genders...just people. It was also the place where my evaluations began to include statements of a personal note. My TSgt at Osan, James J. Riehl wrote, *His devotion to duty, outstanding leadership, and exceptional supervision abilities make SSgt Johnson one of the truly outstanding and professional NCO's that I have had the privilege to be associated with.*

In addition to my immediate supervisors, I got the attention of Lt. Col. William J. Stilger of the 6314th Supply Squadron to which I was attached. He wrote, *SSgt Johnson meets all the criteria under the Air Force Whole Man concept.* (Whole Man was a measuring stick by which those who worked extra hours, volunteered, and maintained a generally well-rounded sense of self were promoted accordingly.) Those, and other words like them began to take on more importance to me than the 100% efficiency ratings. You see, I could memorize equipment manuals and find "lost" money with my eyes closed. That was easy for me and afforded me a nomination for PACAF (Pacific Air Force Command) Supply Airman Achievement Award. It was the transformation of my person that I began to measure with the idea of limitless improvement alongside the technical mastery of my job.

Stateside Again...Education on my mind

From 1968 to 1972 my new little family and I were stationed at Altus AFB in Oklahoma. Yes, I did take some time out to get married to Gracie the 25th of March 1968. She and her daughter joined me and later, we would welcome a son into the world, but more about that a little later in the story.

Altus afforded me the opportunity to further my education at Altus Junior College and Western Oklahoma State where I received my first degree, and A.A. in Social Science. Over the years, I would amass more than 234 curriculum hours in psychology, public speaking, communications, management with human relations in leadership, military justice, history, personnel training, physical training, and world affairs all within the Air Force's various training programs.

Interesting changes in technology occurred while I was stationed at Altus. The advent of computer science and operations began to really take hold and I was very much at the right place, at the right time to take full advantage of learning and implementing computer technology in the supply chain. I was commended for my knowledge of the UNIVAC 1050-II computer system which resulted in faster service with fewer errors in all areas.

Word must have got around that I was pretty good at keeping track of things and so it happened that the entirety of The 443rd Mil ALFT WING would be moved from Tinker AFB to Altus AFB in August of 1969. This included the new C-5A Aircraft training mission. I was charged with providing close coordination with the WSLO (Weapon System Logistics Officer) and C-5A personnel. On top of all that, we had to accommodate the phase-out of the B-52's and the 18th Munitions Maintenance Squadron.

For this and other work, I was nominated for Supply NCO of the year while I completed a Supply System Management Course (6242-1 Officer Training Course at Lowery AFB in Colorado at the technical training school. Mind you, in 1970, "technical training school" was no more than a small room with some desks and manuals. We didn't actually get to work on any machinery at all until we returned to base with a manual and some notes written down that didn't make much sense until we got our hands into it.

It was noteworthy that during this time, Col. James Sandman (a 1948 graduate of Military Academy at West Point) nominated me to fill in while Captain Allan was absent. Taking charge as an NCO was something I would later realize would result in my first Oak Leaf Cluster.

While still with the 443rd at Altus AFB, I earned the rank of Technical Sergeant in November of 1968 and then in January of 1972, I was finally able to join the ranks of Master Sergeant. If it had not have been for my superior officers consistently writing on my behalf in my evaluations, I am not sure I would have made these jumps. Sometimes, I felt like I had to work extra hard to earn what my Caucasian contemporaries were awarded. But, then again, that was another time and place. Still, it was always good to read statements from people like Lt. Colonel Edward Guymon who wrote, "His efforts have greatly contributed to the overall management of the equipment at this base and he should be promoted along with his contemporaries." Before departing Altus, I got the attention of Colonel George M Wentsch who said of my work, "Without question, I recommend him for immediate promotion." (10 September 1971).

With that kind of support, I was finally able to earn my First Oak Leaf Cluster AF Commendation. And then, as with many young men of the era, I found myself on a slow transport to Vietnam.

Almost MAC HQ

My work had been noticed. Furthering my education was not only encouraged by my superiors, it was demanded. There was a proposal in the works with the upper level command to simplify the changes to the Tool Kits which would, as I had written it, save time and money. I was beginning to see real positive results from my hard work. Gracie and I had a good life with our children. It seemed things were headed in the right direction to further my career.

When Colonel George M. Wentsch with the 443rd Military Airlift Wing at MAC (Scott AFB) concurred with my commanding officers at Altus that I was, "an outstanding leader and technician" and "without question" recommended me for immediate promotion the disruptions in my plans began to make themselves known. Upon receipt of my promotion papers at the personnel division at Randolph AFB (Texas), it was determined I had not participated in a sea tour to Southeast Asia for what was called Operational Readiness in the Pacific. It was a choice. I made that choice and said yes, so that's how I got to Vietnam. Here again, this was serious business, not any lackadaisical stuff from a country club and all that, this was serious.

Life interrupted...Vietnam

They say that life changed for everyone who landed in Vietnam during the war. I was no different-on a couple of levels. Although I never saw frontline combat, Tan Son Nhut in August of 1972 was busy with personnel implementing the Vietnamization efforts to reduce the numbers of Americans involved in the war. It was also a time of great racial change. While I was there, I witnessed a lot. Although I can't say I was in any imminent danger, I did arrive in time for the infamous Christmas Bombing, which is something I won't ever forget. And, I may have been late to the party, but I would actually be among the last to leave with a variety of new tools in my toolbox.

Now, during that Vietnam thing, there was a lot of outside stuff going on. There was a lot of racial stuff. I can still hear Marvin Gaye singing, *What's Goin' On?* That was the time when the guys had the Afros. I never accommodated an Afro. It was very tense among senior people and the younger airmen about the Afro. They would get in front of the BX and do all this stuff. It was mostly their form of protesting, which was something going on all over the world at this point, race relations being what they were. I was asked by the wing commander if I would go to them, try to talk some sense into both sides. Maybe even bring two sides to a better understanding of one another. He was going to take me out of my regular job, my professional job, with the supply squadron. He wanted me to become a counselor for trying to make integration work.

The challenge, I guess, as I reflect back on it, when you are trying to broker young groups, young people, into trying to harness their thinking, and trying get them on the right track was a challenge. I got to considering how I might be perceived in that role-how those kids might look at me. In trying to deal with whites and blacks at the same time, I became, if you like-a name for me-like an Uncle Tom. My good name, how hard I had worked for it was too important to me and I didn't want to have that label. That's why I chose to tell the people who asked me to do it to let me out of it and let me go back and do my job. It couldn't have been more than a few days all told, but I sure did pick up a lot of stuff to go in my toolbox from that short experience.

Up until now, equipment management, supply chains, training, repurposing, tracking down missing parts, and generally shoring up the accounting of military materials had been a part of my daily routine. It was my job and I was given ample time to complete my job even if I did often choose to spend extra hours at it. I mean, my crew and I moved an entire AFB full of equipment from one base to another with honors. That sort of gave me some real credibility. Due to my late arrival to the closing ceremonies of the Vietnam conflict, my duties became some of the most intensive and fast-paced supply missions of my career.

I served as NCOIC, Equipment Management Branch for the 377th Supply Squadron while engaged in support of air operations against an opposing armed force at Ton Son Nhut in Saigon. This was also called "Pentagon West" since this was where all the major decision makers were housed. Inside this "Pentagon West" was "Commando Cave" which was decked out with lots of fancy equipment and beautiful furniture. My task at that time was to make sure that we accounted for all that stuff. In the end, some of it was given to the Vietnamese and some of the stuff we kept. Those desks and chairs and all that fancy office equipment were going to be sent back. I was in charge of getting that ready to go.

While there, I was responsible for over 5,000 line items of equipment valued in excess of 38 million dollars, consisting of 359 Custody Receipt Accounts and with assets physically located in approximately 2000 buildings and structures at Tan Son Nhut Air Base, Bien Hoa Air Base, and throughout the Republic of Vietnam.

To say that I walked into a real mess was an understatement. There was equipment and assets scattered all over with billing records that had to be revalidated. In the end, I recovered more than two million dollars in government property and managed to redistribute more than two million dollars in excess equipment to other USAF Organizations. My Commander, Major William W. Vickers wrote of my service, "Sergeant Johnson was personally involved in many classified projects involving the phasedown of the largest USAF equipment account in Vietnam."

In October of 1972, it was announced that a peace agreement was imminent. Prior to that moment, we had just THOUGHT we were in high gear. Major Vickers made note that, "Sergeant Johnson took aggressive action to insure that the redistribution and transfer of 108,619 units of equipment in use valued at $37,440,603 was facilitated in order to insure an orderly phasedown upon the announcement of a peace agreement being signed."

With a peace agreement signed, I had 60 days from 28 January 1973 to close the Base Supply Account. This meant working closely and coordinating with

US Advisory and Vietnamese Air Force personnel. During that timeframe, more than 20 million dollars in accountable assets were either transferred to the Republic of Vietnam or redistributed to other United States installations throughout the world.

Major Vickers took the time to note in my review, "He was one of the last to depart the Republic of Vietnam. The exemplary leadership, personal endeavor and devotion to duty displayed by Sergeant Johnson in this responsible position reflect great credit upon himself and the United States Air Force." He recommended me for the Bronze Star.

Because Major Vickers and some of my other superior officers took the time to present me as worthy of award, I was to see both a Second Oak Leaf Cluster Commendation Medal and a recommendation for the Bronze Star Medal for my service in The Republic of Vietnam from August of 1972 to March of 1973.

Thailand...not quite finished yet

In order to continue advancing up through the ranks, I needed a few more months of active service in the Pacific. It's just the way things were, so I continued to serve as the NCOIC of Supply Surveillance, which sounds pretty official. Plus, there was a great deal at U-Tapao Airfield that needed audited, cleaned up, and set straight before I could leave in good conscience.

I continued to get along with my peers, audited for discrepancies, published directives, and resolved operating and supply customer problems. While I was there, our 635th Supply Squadron was awarded "Best Supply in 13 Air Force" award. SMSgt Jesse F. Pence wrote, "He assisted Recreational Services and other organizations during short periods of TDY and resolved logistics problems of major importance to the directed combat mission and welfare of personnel." This would also be the second time I was recognized for promoting equal opportunity treatment for all personnel. Prior to leaving, Colonel John, G. Ignarski of the 635th Supply Squadron suggested my promotion should follow. "MSgt Johnson's outstanding knowledge and professional competence significantly contributed to this organization's support of the SEA war effort."

Eventually, I got all 182 days required of me and got to head home.

Pen and Ink Changes...words from Randolph AFB

Upon my return from overseas, I discovered that some of my suggestions to improving how the Consolidated Tool Kits should be revised had been considered and a response was determined. Despite the accolades and a clear plan to improve how the tool kits operated, the powers-that-be had decided limiting the number of change requests to the tool kits, as I had suggested, was not to pass. However, I was formally thanked for my participation in the Military Suggestion Program.

For my relatively short tenure associated with Randolph, I did manage to make a good impression within the division. During the absence of the Recruiting Group Logistics Division Officer, Guy V. Allen, Colonel James G Sandman, Commander of the 3506 USAFRG (ATC) appointed me, a Master Sergeant at the time, to assume the position of the Group Logistics Division Officer. Col. Sandman wrote, "Sergeant Johnson is quick to take initiative and is imaginative and resourceful. He sparked important improvements in his division's operations, making it more responsive to the needs of the mission and of the field recruiters. Recommend promotion."

I was thanked by my Captain Chief of the Logistic Division, Guy V. Allen Jr. for filling in during his absence and successfully implementing a project to relocate six detachments headquarters from commercial facilities to military installations.

I guessed I still had something to learn about how to maintain a tool kit, but I was well on my way to establishing myself as a good manager of goods, services, and, most importantly, people.

Reenlistment and Big Spring, TX

With close to 20 years under my belt, it was pretty much what you call a "no-brainer" to reenlist. I was fresh from Vietnam, and with the culture being what it was, remaining on base at Webb Air Base was probably the best option. Staying in the Air Force also meant that I could complete the education that I had started. Or, at least build on what I already had under my belt. I signed the papers on the 30th of May 1973 and watched for what would come my way.

While I was there, I continued on with my work on The Consolidated Tool Kits and even designed a local computer program that gave status on items requisitioned. I continued exploring the idea of Equal Opportunity even though my methods were less "vocal" than the demands and protests going on outside our boundaries. As a MSgt, I was actively involved in the Air Force Equal Opportunity Program and did my best to garner change while remaining a soldier.

Despite my short tenure at Webb, I continued to collect accolades that supported my promotion with Colonel Whitcomb O. Jones writing, "His initiatives guarantees success in this position which directly supports the Webb mission." It wasn't too long before I packed up my family and headed to California.

Mather Air Force Base...California here we come!

With reenlistment came a change of duty. As of 14 June 1974, I was responsible to the Group Logistics Officer at Mather and served as the Group NCOIC. I was charged with formulating procedures and providing operational guidance in related areas to six Air Force Recruiting Detachment Headquarters and 145 recruiting offices throughout 15 states. There was a great deal of commanding involved during the work day but, I was also an active member for the Base Enlisted Advisory Council which helped me give a voice to the enlisted men.

Under my guidance, the group went from six detachments, covering nine states to seven detachments, covering fifteen states that included Alaska and Hawaii. I was commended for my work in planning a Group recruiting support conference that involved preparing a three-day agenda, transportation, lodging, meals, and entertainment. The Major General, B.L. Davis wrote, "MSgt Johnson has demonstrated superior performance and displayed exceptional leadership and management ability in developing one of the best logistics sections in Recruiting Service."

During the first year of my tenure at Mather, I completed 24 more academic hours towards my Bachelors Degree and the course requirements for USAF NCO Academy. Education was fully the bulk of my toolbox at that point in my career and there seemed to be no cure for my desire to learn except for to learn some more.

Formal education was a definite perk with regard to having reenlisted. Recruiting was tedious and political. As a Master Sergeant, it put me in the position to go in and maintain order and solve problems. Not every MSgt had Generals concur as to their integrity, but I worked hard and enjoyed the words written about my work and character. "MSgt Johnson is a hard charging, can do type NCO who has performed exceptionally well in a demanding business. His demonstrated abilities and unlimited potential warrant promotion," wrote Major General Andrew P. Iosue. His words, along with a concurrence by Colonel James G. Sandman set the tone for my final push to excel before I retired from service.

By June of 1976, the country was enjoying a surge of patriotism and I had completed my Bachelors Degree in social sciences as well as the Command NCO Academy. I had applied for graduate school and was well on my way to preparing for life after service. But, despite the accolades, I was stuck at MSgt and hoping for a change to Senior Master Sergeant.

Retirement 1 June 1977- 23 years of service to my country

In the end, I would be selected as a Senior Master Sergeant from the 3506th Group, Air Force Recruiting Service. I had earned four Air Force Commendation Medals, completed my undergraduate studies, and NCO Academy. It was a good run. I saw lots of our good earth, met more people than I could ever have imagined had I stayed on the cotton farm, and held so many conversations that would change the course of my life.

Speaking to the timelessness of social changes, worldwide, global, I think, and I believe; this is my personal opinion, is that when the blacks in America decided that they were going to do something about their living conditions, that was picked up, that was a movement that shed a lot of light to people in other countries. And as we see countries rioting that we have never seen or heard of before, that was the movement that began the international unrest - for lack of a better word. There is a lot of unrest in the world.

Overwhelmingly, my superior officers wrote time and again on my behalf recommending promotion. Those were different times during which the rules varied greatly depending upon the color of your skin. Instead of wallowing in some sort of counterproductive self-pity, I just kept on making myself useful with my ear turned towards the conversations going on around me all the while gathering new tools that would come in handy in the future.

MVT: Saving time and extending yourself is invaluable training.

Chapter 5
Public Education Tour of Duty
Sacramento, Tacoma, New York City

"When I was a child, I spoke like a child, I thought like a child, I reasoned like a child. When I became a man, I gave up childish ways." Corinthians 13:11

The transition from military life to civilian life was one of discovery for myself and for my family. My son, Daryl had his own set of challenges attending a mostly white school and Gracie was teaching in a mostly white setting as well. Being at Mather, really set the tone because I was really interactive within the community. Even though I was still on active duty, I was very involved with civilian activities in Sacramento so, it was not difficult to transition from the military to civilian life. There were also a lot of retirees there so I just kind of eased right into civilian life.

In addition to all that I learned in the military, my membership in groups like the Tuskegee Airmen and my fraternity, Alpha Phi Alpha would shape the direction and philosophies I would utilize for a lifetime. I joined many boards where I knew my presence would not only further my own causes and career, but make a difference in the community in which I lived.

Trying to figure out where I wanted to actually work sent me on a path that made me appreciate freedom in a whole new light. I started out as a volunteer at something they called the Girls' School. It was a lock-up; they could not come and go as they wanted. They had to answer for every move they made.

If they had to go to the bathroom, there was a procedure that kept them from enjoying real freedom or privacy. They ate when they were told to, they were marched here, there, and everywhere. The whole setup was pretty intense. The girls' school, and it's contained environment made me wonder why such an incarceration period did not deter these young women from repeating the same crimes that had landed them there in the first place. The situation, the job, would be the first place that brought the idea of recidivism into the forefront of my mind.

While I was there, as a volunteer, I was offered the opportunity to become a probation assistant, counseling incarcerated juveniles. I couldn't have known that Juvenile Hall would be so educational, especially when it came to the high rate of recidivism. It was like those kids were going out the back door and returning through the front door in very short order. It bothered me. It made me think there must be something more that could be done to intervene before kids got hooked into a life of incarceration.

My work as a counselor was rewarding and it seemed, by the comments of my superiors, that I was doing a good job of it. I guess I never could shake the perception by people that I would make a good counselor. People saw me as good at defusing situations and so that is what I sort of leaned toward.

Working at Juvenile Hall meant that I would go at 8 and get off at 4. Seemed like a sweet deal, the reality was, I was just as locked up as they were for 8 hours a day. So, I'm saying to myself, in the meantime, 'I don't want to be locked up every day for eight hours, or whatever the shift would be, so, I'm going to pursue something else.' It just so happened that, in some of the classes I was taking, there were people there from regular education. We got to chatting about it, about the situation, and they suggested I should get into the public system. I already had a counseling degree in probation, so that was transferable over to the school system. Those folks, just by starting a conversation about my work helped me to move from the penal side to the preventative side, which turned out to be much more my style. My toolbox was full of applicable tools for the situations that would come up and I think, the nature of the tools I picked up in the military were well suited for use in public education.

It was interesting to me that in all the time I spent in the military, I did what was expected of me, I lived where I was told, I slept where I was assigned, I ate at the right times, and filled out the right papers. It was structured, but never like a prison. It was structured so I felt safe enough to take risks with my work and education. It taught me about how the right amount of structure is a good thing, but too much structure, the kind you get when you break too many rules, is not a good thing at all.

Lockup is much tougher than the military ever thought to be and I was glad to put that nugget of information in my toolbox. It came in handy in later years when I needed to, somehow, convince juveniles that structure, rules, and authority were tools that kept peace, fostered learning, and allowed forward advancement. The prevention of recidivism became a passion point for me.

Going into education was also something my wife agreed with as a very good idea. It was Gracie who ultimately suggested that we finally get on "the same schedule". I mean, she was a teacher and we had never been able to take any advantage of holidays together. It made sense, so I set about pursuing a job in education." The two things, reaching kids to reduce recidivism and finally having real family time were the deciding factors in my entrance into education. I wasn't to know that it would be harder than most of anything I ever did in the military. The military was mostly managing parts and paperwork. Education involved managing people. Somehow, the tools I learned in managing military supplies worked nicely when it came to learning how to manage kids and the staff that taught them.

During all of this time following my Air Force retirement, I attended Chapman College. While I was there, I counseled students at the college as well as instructing and counseling at Bauder College in Sacramento. It was a busy time and full of personal growth. This all took place in the time period of 1976 to 1978. It was a time of great changes in our country. We were celebrating our bicentennial and we elected a Democrat from the Deep South, Jimmy Carter as President. Race relations were still tense, but times were definitely changing.

Middle School...a different beat

My career in the public schools began with counseling middle schoolers at Sutter Middle School and California Middle School in the Sacramento Unified School District. California Middle School. This was the premier middle school and was where all the important people had their children. People like Congressmen Vic Fazio and Bob Matsui come to mind when I remember influential families at California Middle. I got to meet lots of people there in guidance and as a result, got financial support, field trips to the capitol, and all the things the average school would not have been privy to. It was a matter of using my tools to start conversations that led to getting the best I could for the students who attended there.

Middle School was very challenging. Middle School youngsters don't know if they want to be an adult or if they want to be a kid. As the counselor or the administrator, you take up the milk money, take them to the bathroom, there's a lot of things that you need to deal with. In most cases, in the elementary, the teachers are young, in Middle School as well. They need lots of expectations from the administration, from the students, and from the parents. But it goes both ways, you have to teach the teachers how to maintain expectations from the students, their parents, family, the community, and so on.

There has to be accountability from all areas surrounding a child if they are to grow up with expectations for themselves. Students have to be just that, students. They have to be people who learn that learning doesn't end at the school doors or with graduation. They have to learn from their community that everyone needs to be a lifelong learner, to be open to gaining as much wisdom from elders, and from peers as they can pack into their brains and hearts. Knowing stuff isn't enough. To become a servant-leader, someone who can share the tools they have collected with others, for the benefit of all means being surrounded by servant-leaders. That has to be taught, even to adults, but not by getting in their face, you have to lead by example.

It was funny to me, here I was, a successful Air Force retiree, going back to elementary school and middle school right along with my son. It was where I learned to hone the skills and tools that I had collected in the Air Force for use in education. Daryl went to school in the San Juan District at Twin Lakes Elementary. Let me share this, I went through Kindergarten to 6th grade for a second time because of Daryl. I volunteered a lot in the school system and got to know principals, teachers, went on field trips with them. I learned about education - certainly at those school levels. It was considerably different than my experience in elementary school all those years ago in Flora, Mississippi, much different. And Gracie, she found it very different too.

Promotion

It must have done me some good to be in elementary school and college at the same time. Pretty soon, I found myself on a fast track to promotion, something I wasn't all that familiar with in the military. In education, in the late 1980's to early 90's, things were moving along much differently for a man of color such as myself. I served California Middle School as a Vice Principal from 1985-1987. From there, I moved to Kit Carson Middle School as principal where I served from 1987 to 1990.

During those years, I continued the community outreach I had started in the military. As a part of the Base Enlisted Advisory Council, I had learned to connect with the community on behalf of the Airmen at Mather. Just like the military, a school system can't exist on its own. There has to be outside support from businesses, homeowners, parents, grandparents, foundations, and a whole host of other resources in order for it to fully support the generation of learners inside.

Meeting Rudy Crew...

In September of 1989, a friend of mine, Dr. Rudolph Crew took the job as Superintendent of the Sacramento Unified School District where he served until June of 1993. I had met Rudy early on because his children and Daryl went to school together so we had interaction through our families. When he became Superintendent, things began to accelerate for my career. It was the beginning of an adventure in education that would eventually allow me to use the majority of the tools I had collected in my box.

Luther Burbank High School...a challenge and a blessing

Why me? I was chosen to go to Luther Burbank by my boss-and my friend. It was through that most powerful tool, conversation, that I was able to make a case for my taking on the mess that was Luther Burbank High School in 1990. I knew all the right people, and what was happening there was the school was basically, literally on fire, so-to-speak. I knew I could put the fire out because I was dedicated to wanting to do that. The word recidivism echoed in my thoughts and I knew there was a need for it. I think the enrollment at that time was 1600 and when I left it was back up to about 2000+. The situation at Burbank was exactly the kind of challenge that I had been preparing for all of my adult life.

Through conversation with Rudy, we established I was already in the system. He had been the deputy superintendent, and then the superintendent. Through our discussion about schools and high schools I asked him if he would consider letting me go to Burbank because they had had about 3 different administrators there within 5 years. And they had problems, problems, problems, problems... so, I told him that I would like to go and be the new principal. He chose me to go and I chose to go.

Becoming the principal of a school in crisis, you think it was a challenge, but it was a blessing in disguise. Knowing a lot of people, influential people, would turn out to be the biggest and most valuable tool in my box.
The mission statement of Luther Burbank High School reads: To create community, appreciate diversity, teach civic responsibility and prepare

students to work, learn and thrive. That first part, to create community, was key to turning Burbank around. The school was located on Florin Road. This was not what you might call an affluent area. The business community consisted mostly of car dealerships that had a very poor opinion of the students. Broken window, vandalized cars, vagrancy... you name it, they were pretty angry about it. The relationship needed turned around, so I just started visiting. Visiting with folks was something deep into my soul and I pulled from my experiences in Flora. It wasn't lost on me that the name Florin was somewhat similar to Flora either. Sometimes, there are little hints in the details.

So, I visited with the community stakeholders, the people that actually had ownership in the community, the business owners. It would take a little more time to convince the students that they also had a stake in the community, so I thought it best to begin with the car dealerships. It turned out to be all right. They were willing to take a chance on me, and, in turn, on the students at Burbank. I convinced them to take down the signs that read, "No Burbank Students". Once the business owners took the deal, I just had to convince the students, faculty, and families to hold up their end of a bargain I had struck on their behalf, without their knowledge.

Reciprocally, those dealerships offered monetary support in terms of outside speakers for us. One dealership had a relationship with the Sacramento Kings and they provided tickets as incentives. We used their vehicles for events. Some of the others would donate money or floats for parades. They added to the auditorium. We had a beautiful auditorium, when it began to leak and the walls became all ugly, they had that taken care of. We had new curtains put in there. So, it was a real reciprocal thing with me. I helped with keeping their car dealerships nice and presentable and they helped the school to look good. We had a very dynamic relationship with the Florin Road Car dealerships.

Knowing what I knew about people, I just started conversations and then listened. I listened to the faculty and made changes. Yes, I did invite certain members to leave; some eventually, some immediately. I replaced them with the kind of people who wanted to teach, to make a difference. After that, it was time to clean house.

The first things to go were the lockers. I had them all removed. I did get a little bit of flack from some of the students, and some of the parents, but, overall, that eliminated lots of problems. People going to their lockers, being late to classes, and also starting incidents because of those lockers made it clear to me that the lockers had to go. So, I took 'em all out. With no place to hide anything, troubles began to go away. The next move I made was to invite several students to leave. They were alternative school material and that was where they would best be served.

After listening to students with an open mind, I discovered safety was a huge issue for them. They couldn't back down and be a part of the solution unless they were safe. In other words, you had to act tough in order not to be victimized. Luther Burbank was sort of an open campus with all sorts of entryways into the school. There were outsiders and it was close to an apartment complex-right off a railroad track and people just walked right through the campus. People who didn't belong there were constantly coming on the campus, so what happened is we just locked the campus down. We had one way in and one way out.

We had a very nice auditorium. It was a beautiful, beautiful building, but it was not being operated correctly. We pared down the entrances and exits. I had an SRO-school officer that was there full time.

And when we had events, it was only for our students. You had to have a ticket in order to get in. Before, people were just coming in and causing problems. So, I went in and shut it down. Started over.

Community Investment...a very helpful tool

So, up until this point, I had been going to meetings, joining boards, doing good along with the community. The schools I had been administering didn't really need much in the way of community investment. The families, the parents of those kids were well connected on their own and my job had been pretty easy when it came to the "things" that make a school better. But Burbank, they didn't have much of anything.

We did not have a football field for the school and, like it or not, football and all that is attached to it is pretty important in high school. This was during the time of Prop 13 that limited taxes. Well, when you limit taxes, budgets get cut and Burbank was right in the middle of an area that was impoverished. When the budgets got cut, and I mean severely cut, things like football fields were the first to go. When Prop 13 came through, they said something like, "you know, you're gonna have to fend for yourselves." All we had was a field and some chalk to mark our field and that's what we were expected to do.

A high school without a sense of community, a place to play, to watch a game and the band was not my idea of building up a school. You have to have academics, art, and activities to keep students busy. Busy students don't get into trouble. So, I figured it was time for me to begin calling on the relationships I had been building in Sacramento since before I retired from the Air Force. There were plenty of people who had known me in the military and as a civilian. I went visiting some more.

Soda Goals and Alternative Tools

So, there was a beverage company, I think it was 7-Up, they would put up a goal for the school in exchange for which they could put their merchandise on the campus. I was told that I couldn't do that. I talked to Rudy (Crew) and Rudy said something bad...'go ahead and do what you need to do'. I went ahead and made an agreement with 7-Up, I think it was 7-Up and they put in the goal posts and scoreboard. From that start, Luther Burbank would begin to feel a better sense of community. Any time something new goes up, something impressive and expensive, like a scoreboard and goal posts, people notice and begin to take a little more interest that verges on the beginnings of pride. Without pride in something, without a place to "belong", a community will not come together for the higher good. You have to give people a place and good reason to gather.

From our humble beginnings of locker removals and goal posts, word spread about the new sheriff in town. And I continued to visit with the community leaders, not only on behalf of the school, but also on behalf of the community.

Time with Fred Teichert

Luther Burbank High School was my real stepping-stone into becoming actively involved in the community. Sure, there was the experience the Advisory Council at Mather, but it was meeting Fred Teichert that really got the ball rolling for me. He approached me at a little restaurant on Florin Road called The Stagecoach, that's where we had our first conversation.

Fred's pet project was bringing a Boys and Girls Club to Sacramento. In a state like California, it was inconceivable that there would be no Club. From what I understood, it wasn't that the Club didn't want to become established in Sacramento, it was a lack of drive and leadership. It was my visibility within the Luther Burbank area that got me involved in the Boys and Girls Club. Fred's family owned a concrete construction company and was a big name in the area of philanthropy. I was poised to set my sights on some of that generosity on behalf of Luther Burbank High School. Little did I know, Fred had his sights set on my help to get the Club established. It all began with a simple conversation-a tool we both valued.

I ended up serving on his board. In fact, I was the #2 person when it came to finding a location for the initial Boys and Girls Club in Sacramento. They have two Clubs serving the kids in the Sacramento Area now. As it turned out, Fred had a passion for combating recidivism that was equal to my own. The establishment of the Club was one very effective and proven way to combat recidivism. Together, we'd like to think we did some good and he remains a big influence in my life.

SMUD (Sacramento Municipal Utility District

Every good school has to have strong ties to local employers. SMUD was one of the biggest employers in the area, so I set out to capture some of the benefits that a utility could provide our students at Luther Burbank.

I found that I could trade out being principal for the day with the head honcho, David Freeman, at SMUD. He learned something about students and I got my foot in the door. Soon enough, we had kids working summer jobs at SMUD. The management began to spend time with our students teaching them basics of what it is like to have a job. They learned real world economics, business and financing, and engaged with people who could answer their questions about the world of work. It was a good trade.

The Law and Luther Burbank

Being that so many of our kids had historically been familiar with the punitive side of the law, we thought it a good idea to introduce them to the enforcement point of view. In May of 1993, Superintendent Rudy Crew received a memorandum outlining our proposed 4th and 5th R's (Rights and Responsibilities) program.

Through that program, we received a grant in the amount of $1500 to provide a course in government in partnership with the Unity Bar Association and the McGeorge School of Law Student Bar Association. The partnership provided positive role models across the ethnic and gender spectrum. Students worked with local attorneys and judges in the classroom and took outings to small claims court, highway patrol headquarters, and homeless shelters. The impact of such a program was vital in our push to reduce the rate of recidivism in our justice system. It all starts with the schools and the community. You have to bring all the players together for a good conversation no matter what their skin looks like or how they speak. It all starts with conversation.

The Mayor comes to school

Mayor Joe Serna found our school to be of interest with all the goings-on. We invited him to tour our campus and meet the students. He penned a short letter that not only came from his point of view as mayor, but also as a professor of government at CSUS. He said, "It was a wonderful opportunity for me to see what a difference you, your staff, students and the community have made to turn your school around." He went on to explain how gratifying it was to see the "wholesome and warm relationship between you and your student body and the positive climate of your campus."

It is words such as these that reminded me about the power of a good thank you note. You see, people have to have encouragement, especially when they are in the trenches of a particularly difficult situation. For me, it was always humbling to receive such a note, but it also taught me to write more notes to more people. Little sticky notes, big cards, professional accolades, and so on…the written word is a special kind of conversation worth every moment of your time and effort to send.

And then…I joined the Navy

I brought some thoughts to Luther Burbank from my military toolbox that I could share with the current JROTC commander (at Burbank) that would benefit all concerned. It just so happened the program was based out of The Department of the Navy, so, I changed my thinking just a little, but will remain an Airman for the duration of my time here on this great earth.

Expansion of the program was first on the agenda for both of us. We both felt strongly that the school could and would benefit from a strong JROTC program. I encouraged the commander of the unit to give some presentations, not only to the students, but also to the parents of the student body to increase the number of people that would go into the program. My purpose was to generate some interest into building the number of JROTC students, which we did.

In June of 1993, just before my promotion to Area III Administrator, I received a letter from The Department of the Navy inviting me down to Pensacola for the purpose of participating in their NJROTC instructor training. The N stood for "new" which gave me pause to think hard about the message I would be bringing to those who knew how to operate in the military realm, but might be very new to education. Having been there myself, it was a challenge to decide exactly what to tell them. It is also interesting to note that President Bush (the first) had started an initiative to expand the JROTC program.

The part of my invitation letter that stood out to me read like this:

It is our goal to make our instructors understand how important they are to our team, and what a tremendous impact they have on the lives of their students. While that information will be rewarding to them, we also want to back it up with the practical tools that they will need to use on a daily basis in their respective high schools.

It was that visit to Pensacola and the training seminar at which I instructed that led me to renew efforts in Sacramento to increase our JROTC program by digging deeper into the middle schools. I gathered more tools than I offered at that seminar. My passion for reducing recidivism was also fueled by learning of the success of other troubled school systems that had implemented JROTC in the middle grades. I remember that being one of the first things I tackled in my new role that fall.

Assistant Area Administrator, Sacramento Unified School District

To say that advancement had sped up for African Americans since the early days of my service in the Air Force would be an understatement. It was by no means where it should be, but compared to the track I was on in the military, things were moving along.

Among my first memorandums would be a proposal for a Junior Cadet Program targeted directly towards the middle school population. Memories of a soldier with a blue jacket, a certain math teacher, and my own career in the Air Force led me to believe that enhancing the current present curriculum with added requirements for social behavior awareness, self-awareness, self-esteem and preparation for the world of work in a business community would be in order at the middle school level. I believed in early intervention and I acted on it to steer students in my district towards the self-discipline training offered by the JROTC. After all, I was living proof of a military career changing the course of a person's life.

Upon taking the Area Administrator position, the local news (Pocket News) came out and had a conversation with me. I say a conversation, because it was for a smaller paper that read more like a conversation than an interview. I liked that. The writer, Patricia Clark, wrote up a nice piece that summed up how I felt about moving from a local school position to one where I wasn't in daily touch with the students and teachers. She quoted me as saying,

"I'm dealing with more adults, more district matters and I have less contact with kids. But it is pleasing and challenging, too…I think I'm in a position to make decisions to affect more lives than being at the school site. My experiences at the school sites should be transferred to the people who make policy for all students. That's really what my role is, an advisory role to the district hopefully for the benefit of all students."

I was pleased with the idea that I had been at Burbank long enough to graduate the freshman class that came in when I became principal. When I became Area Superintendent, I think I was over maybe 15 elementary schools and several middle schools and one other high school. The "other" high school was called Kennedy High School and was a premier high school.

One of the most difficult decisions I was charged with making would be whether Luther Burbank was going to be a school of International Baccalaureate - IB School or would the program go to Kennedy. Kennedy ended up with more votes because it was located in a very, very upscale neighborhood predominantly controlled by Caucasians. Even though I felt both schools were deserved of the program, I didn't rock the boat, just moved right on and things worked out ok. I guess it is like that Kenny Rogers song…you gotta know when to hold 'em and know when to fold 'em. I have found a good poker face is an immensely useful tool to keep handy in my personal toolbox.

As I think back on the interview and my time in Sacramento, I remember how I wanted to take the lessons I had learned and the tools that I had honed, and apply them more globally. The move was one that started me on a path towards sharing my toolbox with others, in new places who might be facing similar challenges. It wasn't long before Rudy Crew asked me to join him in an entirely new city that needed fresh ideas and a boost for the school system.

The last letter I have kept in my files as I prepared to end my tenure with the Sacramento Unified School District was one that meant a great deal to me.

Dated March 15, 1994, the Chief of Police, Arturo Venegas, Jr. wrote:

I have enjoyed our working relationship and appreciate your input and assistance in dealing with school-related problems. With today's constant downsizing, it is important that educators be as innovative as possible in their profession. You have been just that and have dealt with problems head-on. I wish you the very best in your new endeavor and look forward to continuing a positive working relationship with Luther Burbank High School.

The words he chose to use helped me to rest a little easier knowing that he would help continue the legacy of Luther Burbank High School as a place of learning, order and safety. I hoped that, together, the community had come to value the high school as a central part of life in the district. I left feeling we had brought the stakeholders together, in ownership of a community that would continue its positive trajectory. During my tenure there, we had some students go on to Ivy League Schools. Some of them are doing quite well now, doctors and attorneys. Some, not all, test scores went up and it became a very civil place.

Rudy, me and a ticket to Tacoma

With the move, came a promotion to Assistant Superintendent Elementary Education of Tacoma Public Schools. This change sent me deep into the early grades where my efforts to tame recidivism would find their way into the classroom. Testing was, of course, high on the list for measuring achievement and Tacoma faced some challenges. But still, as test score rose, so would self-esteem. And self-esteem, I had determined, played an enormous role in the rate of recidivism within the juvenile justice system. Boosting scores meant boosting self-esteem and kids with a healthy outlook were far less likely to find themselves incarcerated.

Upon arrival, we assessed the culture of stereotype and immediately set about changing the mindset of teachers, students, parents, community, and all supporting parties. Again, if there is no ownership, no stakeholders to come to the table, if everyone is operating as if a situation were a lost cause, well, then it will be a lost cause.

I didn't use any magic formula. I simply reached into my toolbox, pulled out the conversation tool and began to talk to people. Although Tacoma was completely new territory for me, I found the tools of change to be the same anywhere I went. Rudy and I worked hard to change the segregated cultures and pushed the fact that children are young and intelligent. They need only be challenged.

My strategy for creating change was much the same as any other time in my life. I made myself visible. I drank coffee with the coffee klatches. I got to know parents, scheduled fun activities for parents and other principle people involved in the life of the students. We enjoyed a good relationship with the Tacoma Tribune and got coverage for our causes. We held contests, awarded small grants, and encouraged investment from all parties. All this work was done to facilitate a relationship for all involved to participate with the schools. As always, it started with a conversation. It really is as simple as that.

Eventually, we got test scores up through a variety of strategies. For one, without teaching to the test, we discovered that students didn't know how to take a test. It seemed a pretty simple fix and, once implemented, scores, predictably, went up. Secondly, but no less important, Rudy believed in children. He might pound a fist on a boardroom table to get the attention of adults, but with kids, he was as gentle as they come. He believed they could do more if their teachers expected more. Again, it was a simple as changing expectations and having a conversation with the students about it. It was a valuable lesson for me that student stakeholders are just as important, if not more, as the adults involved.

New York 1996

Now, Rudy was a pretty recognizable name in the world of education. His skills, his no nonsense manner was sought after by many school districts, but one challenge interested him more than others. A New York native, Rudy was offered an opportunity to serve as Chancellor of the New York City Board of Education. He took the position and asked me to serve as his special assistant. He wanted me to come with him and do what I did best; start conversations.

The New York City school system wasn't political, per se, throughout. Instead, you might call it kind of a close political society. The system had about 1.1 million students, about 1,100 schools, and 32 districts. Each one had a superintendent over those 32 districts. Rudy wanted to make a "33rd", which he did. The 33rd district was comprised of those schools that were performing below grade level. They weren't performing up to the standards, so we made 33 my responsibility. I was to deal with those 13 schools in, I think it was 4 boroughs. Manhattan was pretty bourgeois - or whatever- so it didn't have a lot of problems. It was Queens, Brooklyn, The Bronx, and a little bit of Staten Island that had schools with real cause for concern. But, here again, I - being his special assistant, didn't get into the real weeds of the politics, but always kind of navigated around the politics. The political scene, well, that was Rudy's responsibility.

It was tough; it was a tough place to work. They had this one high school, I don't know how many they have now, but it was called Stuyvesant High School. It's located in Manhattan and is considered a premier school. This is where, at the time, you had to more-or-less have a parent with a sponsor to get students in if you came from, say, the wrong side of the tracks. So, we were faced with an atmosphere that was very politically operated.

Despite the politically charged arena that we had stepped into, I was able to rely on my trusted toolbox to provide me with the reliable tools of our past successes. After all, our successes were the reason New York hired us all the way across the US of A. We had a reputation and it made it somewhat easier to implement the changes that were sorely needed.

In stark contrast to Stuyvesant High School was the high school in the 33rd district... that movie, *The Principal* with Jim Belushi, was just about the closest representation of the condition of that school. The producers of that movie were spot on. I think the worst of it was the rodents-bad, bad, bad-rodents. In fact, the schools were infested with the stink of despair, as if no one cared at all. Situations like that, they require swift and, sometimes, unappreciated hard decisions.

Never, in all of the time I had been a part of the public school system had I seen anything like this. As a matter of fact, I had never seen anything this disgusting and disappointing in all of the time I spent in the Air Force. Nothing compared to this mess. I reached deep into my toolbox and pulled out the big guns. All of the stuff I had accumulated from the military, the probation department, and other organizations was very beneficial to me.

The most underutilized, but most readily organized group were the ministers. This was the mission field if ever I saw one. I used to meet with the ministers as a part of their ministerial alliance. We met, I think about every other month. We'd talk about what was going on in the five boroughs and that kept a lot of heat off of Rudy in terms of the community. That was the biggest part of my job, pulling the community in, explaining what he was doing as Chancellor and why he was doing it. It was strategic warfare with poverty and ignorance as public enemy number one.

For the 33rd district, we got money to upgrade the buildings and exterminate the rodents. In terms of those 13 schools, the infrastructure was deplorable, so we were able to change the face of a lot of those buildings. Through improved leadership choices, we were able to provide better service. As with any new sheriff in town, we had to remove some people and bring in some fresh leaders.

One of the statements he wrote in his book, Only Connect, that resonated with me was about his vision for the twenty-first century:

This means we are all vested, financially if not morally, in helping every one of our fellow citizens to operate at the highest possible level, and public education is the key to that. If the poverty, ignorance, and illiteracy that occur now don't hurt your soul, then they hurt your pocketbook in a million little ways in both the private and public sectors, and, worst of all, they hurt you through the opportunities lost. (Rudy Crew, Only Connect 19)

Rudy Crew has not only been my friend, but it was an honor to work side-by-side with him to clean house in a number of school districts from one coast of this amazing country to the other. Together, we slayed cultural, racial, and economic dragons all in the name of good public education. Neither one of us started out with a silver spoon in our mouths. We worked our way up and out of where we were to where we are now.

The one thing I can say that we had in common, besides humble beginnings, was a loving family. Rudy's dad raised him up with similar values as my parents provided. I think, at the basis, that is why we reached so hard into the community during our time together. Too many kids these days face tough home lives and that affects their self-esteem. Without a strong self-esteem, a child is at risk of fading away. Strong self-esteem is a tool that everyone needs to have in the uppermost tray of their personal toolbox.

Chapter Five MVT: Reach deep into the community on behalf of kids.

Chapter 6
Furthering my own education...from gut to dissertation

Hold on to instructions; do not let it go, guard it well, for it is your
life. Proverbs 4:13

Common Elements in Administration: A Rationale for
Administration as a Profession

If that title isn't a mouthful, I don't know what is. The plain and simple truth about writing a dissertation is that you have to do it in order to earn your doctorate. I earned my Doctor of Philosophy from Pacific Western University. (According to my research, PWU was absorbed into California Miramar University in 2005 or thereabouts.)

Of course, the dissertation wasn't even close to where I began improving my formal education, and it isn't the last place I will learn something, but it does sort of put much of my management style into a format someone might want to read one day. However, my continued formal education beyond high school obviously didn't begin with a dissertation. It was during my tour of duty in Korea, that it became very clear I needed to channel my energy and my talents towards making this whole world a better place. It also became very clear to me that in order to leave this spinning ship in better shape than I found it upon birth, I would need to engage in more education on my own behalf and on behalf of others.

The simple act of teaching English to Korean orphans gave me plenty of food for thought. Even though I had left high school early to enter the Air Force, I was able, through the trajectory of the military, to bridge that gap with advanced education degrees. In fact, getting into the Air Force wasn't really all that easy. Back then, you had to pass tests so the powers that be could judge your aptitude. Somewhere in the back of my mind, I guess I always knew I needed more formal education, but it took reading to orphans with my squadron to bring furthering my education to the forefront of my thoughts.

My station at Altus Air Force Base in Oklahoma would be where I would launch that trajectory of education. Through the initiative, Air University, I was able to move through the non-commissioned officer classes. From 1968 to 1972, I attended classes at Altus Junior College (later became Western Oklahoma State) where I took the basics in English, psychology, math, science, business machines, speech, history, and government classes that resulted in an Associate of Science Degree. For me, that was just the beginning of a life-long hunger for education.

Looking back on those days, I am reminded to say that, while I chose a college education, my original tract wasn't necessarily headed towards academics. My aptitude, my job, and my training had been in supply logistics. The kind of on-the-job training I got in the United States Air Force is exactly what we should be offering so many young people today. Learning a trade is not somehow degrading or lower in status than gaining a college education. Trades are wholly and completely necessary. And what is more, they take hands-on skills that cannot be learned from just a book. I can say THAT with confidence because, when technology first began to take hold of daily life in the military, I was at the forefront of it. We learned the concepts and basic ideas from books and presentations, but it took getting our hands on computers to fully understand the technology and what it could do for us in the supply chain.

What I am really saying here is, while I eventually went for the college degree, I know that it isn't always for everyone. As a society, we seem to have placed too much emphasis on the academic route when the technical route is just as important to our nation, our world as a whole, and we don't seem to value it like we should. Sending students to college when they are not ready, or interested, is setting them up to fail.

I also feel that I need to interject the absolute importance of the junior college. Some high school seniors might be ready to attend a four-year college by their sophomore year of high school, but others might not be ready until they have completed their sophomore year of college. That is where the junior college fits in. A smaller campus, with a concentration of core classes, might be just the ticket for the student who isn't ready, or cannot afford to attend the larger university. For me, the junior college allowed me to complete those core classes on a schedule that accommodated my young family and my Air Force duties. It turned out to be a huge win for me and gave me some perspective on secondary education that I might not otherwise have fully understood as a counselor many years later.

After completing my work at Altus Junior College, I was able to continue my education at Chapman College located in Orange, CA. I was still in the military when I received my B.A. in Social Science. Chapman College was also where I earned my M.A. in Counseling.

With the broad range of psychology and management classes offered, I was able to get a good idea of what kinds of societal ills our human species was facing. One of the things that began to come to light was this idea of recidivism. It seemed that so many of the programs and methods of management within the school system and the juvenile justice system left so much to be done with regard to kids continually returning to the same bad behaviors that had landed them in trouble to begin with. It would become a resounding word in my mind for many years and, in some ways, still fascinates me to some degree even today. I suppose that is why I am so committed to our public school advisory board, the Boy Scouts, and am continually invited to advise charter schools. Somewhere, the revolving door of recidivism must be slowed to a complete stop in order to secure what I consider the blessings of our liberty.

Why do people repeat mistakes? Why don't we learn? How do we throw a monkey wrench in the works and get people off a repetitive tract? These were all questions that would lead me to continue studying and then teaching the classes that had to do with the psychology of the management of people across the board and the various board rooms in which I have spent many hours.

I have led workshops in vocational education, interpersonal relationships, and presented at different conferences for the National Alliance of Black School Educators. I was an instructor/counselor at Bauder College as well as Chapman College where the ideas of recidivism and self-esteem continued to pull at my mind and helped me form the methods I would use at the administrative level within the different school systems where I served.

In 1979, I earned my Doctorate in Management. Management is a broad term for something as simple as getting things done. You need lots of really good tools in your personal toolbox to get anything done and I felt like, by the time I was faced with writing my thesis, my toolbox was pretty full of useful stuff, so I wrote about it.

It all boiled down to the basics of listening to one another. I mean, not talking over one another; having a real conversation with give-and-take. Simplifying a doctoral dissertation may seem to make it less valuable, but I think, if you really have learned what you need to know, you should be able to distill your thoughts down into an easy to digest relevant concept.

My personal opinion came into play and it was written in a line I wrote that management can go across the spectrum. *Regardless of the size or type of group, in order to remain intact, it must be effective in defining its goals and purposes in light of its membership and in achieving those goals. The method for meeting these requirements constitutes what is called organization, management or administration.* Now, all that being said, the simple fact is that in any organization, you have to have leadership in order to prosper, progress, achieve, move forward, accomplish...any and all of that.

Naturally, the sophistication of the administrative process will vary tremendously from the three-member daredevil clubs of children to the large business corporations and the intricate systems of public institutions, even while the principles and philosophy of the administration remain the same.

Again, the idea of basic management has to be distillable into a basic concept capable of serving children's games of jacks, Pokémon cards, or Manhunt all the way to the board room of major corporations or governing entities. The rules of managing the meetings are pretty much the same.

To summarize it, I think being in all manner of different places and interacting with different levels of people all the way from Flora, MS to overseas, and back to the US of A gave me a perspective on managing people and things that can't really be taught in school. The thing is, it really isn't rocket science in the long run. Administration is mostly common sense, which is something I feel our great country is sorely lacking in. I also think one of the key things to management is having a sense of humor. You have to have a sense, an understanding of people, and you have to have some basic psychology.

The kind of basic understanding of people and people's behavior and the culture that you are dealing with is, without a doubt, critical to making things work. I think you can manage and supervise just about any group of people. That's really what my own personal education boils down to. Learn to manage yourself, others around you, your home life, work, recreation, and community involvement.

The world presents so many opportunities to learn to manage what goes on around you. You just have to be open and willing to receive it. Funny thing is, if you don't learn to get along with people, the universe has a way of recycling past lessons until you do learn.

And because the universe has a way of helping you learn lessons, I thought it would be a good idea, as I went along in life, to continue my bible studies. As you can tell from each chapter, the bible has provided me with plenty of good insight, comfort, and guidance throughout my life. The guidance was so good that I found myself leaning towards deeper studies with each decade.

Eventually, I would study to become a deacon. Woodman Hill Baptist, in Flora, was the first church in which I served as deacon. That was during my time in the Air Force. Later in life, I served at Peachtree Corners Baptist Church. I think, my favorite study was for the Bible Study Fellowship. It was an eight year commitment that resulted in a deeper understanding of what it means to minister unto others. For me, a passionate commitment to Christ has been most important to me in my studies. Christ gave all for us and I believe we should freely seek Him.

Education MVT: You need all the education you can get; never stop learning.

Chapter 7
Active Civic and Social Tour of Duty in a new community

Remember not the former things, nor consider the things of old. Behold, I am doing a new thing; now it springs forth, do you not perceive it? I will make a way in the wilderness and rivers in the desert. Isaiah 43:18-19

How do you follow tenure in New York with an influence like Rudy Crew? First, I prayed about it. I thought about the people around me who still needed me and I listened to good counsel from many sides.

As it turned out, my mother began to need more frequent care and visits from me to make sure she was in good shape. Gracie and I had no real interest in returning to any of the places we had lived throughout our somewhat nomadic life, so I began to investigate communities where we both might enjoy retirement as well as offer us easy access to the airport. In 1998, we "landed" in unincorporated Gwinnett County with a zip code showing we were closest to a city called Norcross located in the state of Georgia, USA. Interestingly, we would eventually change the city we were connected to and not even move out of our house. More about that in a bit.

We were close enough to the airport so we could fly back to Jackson to check on family pretty easily. We were also close enough to enjoy some local sports teams. I had season tickets to the Falcons and attended many of the Hawks and Braves games. Our home was in a stable neighborhood with good schools and nice places to gather. We found a church to attend where I served as deacon. It was a really great life. But, I kind of got a little bored.

I had dabbled in real estate, worked with an educational data company, and consulted on some education projects, but with the economy and the post 9-11 world, work was really not something I wanted to do any more. I wanted to consider myself "retired" and I needed a hobby. So, I took out my conversation tools from my toolbox and went out in search of some good conversation.

I have to admit to a little secret here. Most people like to say, "Let's have coffee." That's code for, "Let's have a conversation." Problem is, even with as much coffee as I down in any given day, I really don't like it at all. But, it is a huge part of our social construct in this society and who am I to refuse a cup of coffee if it comes with a side of good conversation? Being able to drink a cup of coffee is a really handy tool to have at your disposal, even if you don't like it.

When it comes to the first places I started to reach out to my new community, I would have to say Rotary was a most efficient way to meet people. Lunch meetings at Rotary had always led me to very effective relationships and I was pretty sure it would continue to serve me well.

I met some people, I began to get the lay of the land, and the places I might fit in began to make themselves clear. My own "new beginning" turned out to be a "new beginning" for my neighborhood as well. The birth of a city from an unincorporated area is no small task. It starts with a vision, comes with some amount of pain, a great deal of hard work, and, eventually, culminates with something amazing that you can watch grow before your very eyes.

My involvement with all the players who made the City of Peachtree Corners happen here in Gwinnett County began, as you might have guessed, with a conversation. At the time, my good friend, Lynette Howard was serving as the president of the United Peachtree Corners Association. She and I kind of hit it off and she pulled me into that circle of people who were moving and shaking the things you have to move and shake in order to accomplish something as BIG as growing a city. One of my best memories is standing with this group behind Governor Nathan Deal as he signed the proclamation declaring us a city. It was a proud moment worth celebrating, but once it was over, there was still plenty of work to be done and that is why I still serve on the Peachtree Corners Downtown Development Authority.

Meeting Lynette led to meeting a whole group of very connected folks in the county. After getting involved with my new city, I ended up being asked to serve on the Housing Authority. Even though I have circled the sun more than 80 times, I manage to continue as the Vice Chairman of the Development Authority of Gwinnett County.

In a county as large as Gwinnett, there is always something to be decided on and it keeps me very busy. Like I said, I am not one to hang out and watch television all day long.

My Rotary connections were directly related to my work with the Northeast Georgia Council of The Boy Scouts of America. This is a group that has my heart. Scouting forms great leaders and I believe in what they do. There are so many young people today without any direction. As a society, we don't seem to ask enough of our very capable youth. Their energies are often wasted because we don't have enough leaders to provide opportunities to learn about the real world.

And because the world isn't complete without good healthcare and our area is blessed with an outstanding hospital system, I got involved. Yes…because of a few well-meaning individuals who thought a guy who looks like me, has a sense of commitment to my community, and generally gets along with others, I ended up on the Gwinnett Hospital Board of Directors.

My good friend, Wayne Sikes, who pulls no punches in expressing himself, decided that the hospital board needed some coloring up and I would be the guy to start a new trend. All kidding aside, it is like I have said before, the county in which I live is very diverse, but we lack representation that reflects that diversity. I am grateful Wayne reached out to me in order to bring diversity to the Hospital Board and I know he continues to make all kinds of efforts to foster diversity in all of the work that he does.

Now, I have established that I had a career in the Air Force, and I was involved with the Navy JROTC during my years in Sacramento at Luther Burbank High School, so it should not come as a surprise that I am also in the Army. I am a proud member of the Salvation Army and, also not a real surprise; I serve on the local Board of Directors for the unit in Lawrenceville, GA. In addition, I serve the Salvation Army Metro Atlanta Area Command as an Ex-Officio member, which is fancy talk for advising the board members.

Both of my roles with the Salvation Army are very important to me. Because I very much believe that "Doing the Most Good" is an appropriate motto, I put a lot of effort into my work there. You see, offering a hand up is completely different than offering a hand out. At the SA, we do help people with a variety of needs, but one of the most important is a program called Home Sweet Home. I am particularly interested in supporting that program because it allows families to remain together when faced with a homelessness situation. It also speaks to me because the resources are both private and public in nature. My experience with the Housing Authority and the connected elected officials combines with my experience with the Salvation Army to help those in need locally.

Another reason I love the Home Sweet Home project is that it doesn't put those without a home into some sort of localized area causing a stigma to be attached to the families, especially the children, which can be associated with homelessness.

There are as many reasons for homelessness as you can possibly imagine. I have witnessed most situations are caused by a bunch of things that can take a family down like dominoes. Adding a stigma, or worse yet, breaking up a family to provide shelter, creates more problems down the line. Home Sweet Home collaborates with private and public resources to help those in need by, you guessed it, Doing The Most Good…and I really like doing just that.

As you might have figured, I stay pretty busy, so age is no excuse for not being involved in your community. There really is no excuse for lack of involvement because everyone, in someway can contribute to the community as a whole. Children, adults, people of all ethnicities, those considered disabled, and so on can all contribute in one way or another.

Despite the diverse nature of each person's own situation, everyone can start a conversation by some means. Conversations start the ball rolling to a better understanding of what is inside a person so we are less likely to stand in judgment of the outside of a person.

Civic and Social MVT: Always do the most good.

Chapter 8
Conversations and Commentary: I get by with a little help from my friends

Walk with the wise and become wise, for a companion of fools suffers harm. Proverbs 13:20

Suffice it to say, when you lead with an introduction, conversation is likely to follow. It would be hard; in fact, it would be impossible to determine which of the conversations I have held in my lifetime would rank as my favorite. There are so many people, from so many of the "tours of duty" in my lifetime who have had some bearing on who I am today that I could not choose a favorite. I think I have enjoyed most of the conversations I have been a party to over the years.

Preparing this book has given me many hours of reflection. All that reflection has led me to an understanding of just how privileged my life has been when revisiting some of the people who represent so many places in my past. I have to say it has been a little like eavesdropping on my own funeral! Now, before you think that is too morbid, so-to-speak, I actually look forward to my promotion to heaven one day. Just not today…or tomorrow. In the meantime, reflection has become an important part of how I go about my days.

I must admit, reading through these interviews, some from when we first floated the idea of a memoir and some more recently, I am humbled. I can say I have been moved to tears and laughter. Each day I keep these friends, and so many others like them, close in my prayers. Without this network, I would not be the person I see in the mirror today.

Over the years, I have shaken hands with thousands of people and I see the crossing of arms to reach into a handshake as part of a web that connects my time in Vietnam to my days on the Housing Authority in a county like Gwinnett in Georgia that is fully representative of the globe I have trotted for eighty years. Our melting pot is in dire need of more conversations and I will continue to be blessed by the work of these people who have chosen to accept my invitation to conversation.

As a matter of arrangement, I have placed folks into my four tours of duty. Jim Peterson probably knew me the best as far as my tour of duty in the Air Force. We served in Vietnam together. He speaks about a time and a place that still remains very vivid in my mind. Not to dwell on it, but vivid all the same.

My education "tour" provided me with a different perspective on management. Before I got started in counseling and administration, my management experiences had been on an adult level. Here, I kind of "got down" to a different level. While they might have been shorter than me, kids provided tremendous lessons on just what is needed to help our youth succeed in this world. So, in a way, they helped me form a better introduction to conversations that would eventually lead to some good problem solving.

One of the biggest problems I saw in my education days was that of recidivism. Like I mentioned before, watching kids go in and out of the revolving door of our justice system was disheartening. These kids were smart, some of them too smart for traditional means of dealing with the problems often presented by youth. Our juvenile justice system was so disconnected from our education system; and still is today. My friend Bob Kelgord mentions our efforts to help the recidivism problem. I think that topic may provide enough material for an entire book in and of itself.

Now, because the better part of my civic and social career has been spent in Gwinnett County, GA, you will find lots of commentary from those I serve with across a variety of platforms. I guess, like the subject of recidivism, diversity in representation is another of my "hot topics". What I found, when I looked around the rooms at so many different functions was that I kind of stuck out just a bit…and not just because I am tall. Instead of shying away from a room full of people who don't look like me, I chose to stick out my hand, introduce myself, and, well you should know by now…start a conversation. Today, those rooms are beginning to look a little bit different, but not near diverse enough. The words written by my friends in civic and social circles are kind and generous. I would not hesitate to write the same of them.

Lastly, is my connection to the first tour in my life; which is about family. I don't have much connection any more to Mississippi, but I do have Gracie and Daryl's words to sort of sum up what it might be like to really have to live with me. In all, I think I came out looking pretty good there. My family is a real blessing to me and I appreciate their kind words.

So, have a read about what others have taken away from conversations with me. If you are of a mind, maybe we might meet one day and can have a conversation of our own. Until then, I can honestly say I am looking forward to meeting more people.

Jim Peterson-United States Air Force (Saigon)

I met LC while we were both serving in the USAF and stationed at Tan Son Nhut Air Base in Saigon, Vietnam from 1972-1973. We were working together in the Supply Squadron when the Air Base came under a motor attack one morning. I received an urgent call from the control tower at the airfield that they needed protective flak vests immediately. I asked for volunteers to accompany me to the flight line, and only LC volunteered. After drawing weapons from the armory, LC and I proceeded in a vehicle with the flak vests and delivered them to the soldiers who were laying prone on the floor when we arrived. No casualties were taken during that time, but it made a distinct impression on me as to the character of LC.

We bonded together not just as fellow soldiers but friends as well. We returned to normal assignment duties after the withdrawal of all combat troops from the country negotiated by Henry Kissinger in Paris the month before. I departed on the last day of combat in March 1973. LC and I often talked about what it was like to be in Jackson at the time of racial segregation, and we promised that one day we would meet there and enjoy our friendship in an integrated Mississippi- which we did!

One of the most remarkable character traits I found with LC was his iteration with his subordinates who looked up to him as a senior NCO. They knew they could confide in him about personal and professional matters, and that he would help them. If he sensed that someone was having an issue or problem he would informally open conversations with them to allow them to open up. He had all the "tools" he needed to maintain his reputation as a sterling example of a professional NCO and person, and an example for others to emulate then and now.

LC has a "can do" attitude in resolving issues be it with people or situations. He cares about those he works with which is recognizable when someone talks to him on a personal or professional basis. I am happy that he still calls me his friend after all these years. We have a mutual respect and I truly admire him as a person who has overcome adversity and discrimination while growing up in Mississippi and later in the military.

Fred Teichert (Sacramento, Boys & Girls Clubs)

We met in Rotary when LC was principal at Luther Burbank High School. We were in the early stages of planning for a Boys and Girls Club in the area that surrounded the high school. He was very knowledgeable about the area and I saw that as an asset. At my request, he hosted a group of planning people at Luther Burbank. Back then; we were the largest city without a Boys and Girls Club, and it was sorely needed (1994 or so).

We had a possibility for some block grant money and LC literally drove every block to find the best lot in the area. He was instrumental in selecting the site. Unfortunately, the building didn't get built for another ten years, so LC didn't get to see much of what he had set in place. In the meantime, we were able to build a smaller club in downtown Sacramento.

He had been in the Air Force before entering education and I think a very nice way of putting things is that he made people think they want to do something whenever he asked them to do it. He made you want to do what he asked without ever bossing anyone around.

Prior to our efforts for the Boys and Girls Club, The Salvation Army had tried to put a center in. It was a very challenged area of town and there was nothing for kids. They needed a place they could come to do their homework, play sports, do art and so on. LC saw that this was what the kids in the Luther Burbank neighborhoods really needed. They needed support to make it as human beings and in school. He was at Luther Burbank during a period when there was a recession so money was tight. LC made sure that by hook or by crook, those kids got what they needed.

He spoke to area congregations and got people to do homework with them (the kids). It was one of those things where people were fearful of teenagers, but the kids who went to the Boys and Girls Clubs kept things clean. The Club was important to us because you would see these tough street kids come through the door and set their outward appearances away. These were kids who still had not learned simple things like how to take turns. LC helped change that.

Over the years, even after he moved on to Tacoma, New York, and Atlanta, LC and I have had some great conversations. We developed a good friendship. He could be pretty tough. Political divisions within his neighborhood were tough. He took on challenging council members with tools from his toolbox. LC knew where to set boundaries and not be a pushover. He was diplomatic in a sense that everybody got to process information and make their own decisions. If people crossed lines, he never took the bait. Somehow, he managed to bring situations around to the best thing for kids and rally people around ideas.

Over the years, he made himself available to tour with public agencies and I always felt he respected my time. He is somebody who is right there in the trenches with you.

Robert Kelgord (Sacramento)

One of the most important aspects in efforts to combat juvenile recidivism is the influence of teachers while juveniles are in some type of custody. In Sacramento County, we were very fortunate to have a fine faculty at our various institutions (all of which, except one, are now closed). I had the privilege of watching LC in his classroom performance and in the high personal standards that he maintained, exemplifying the importance of non-criminal conduct.

Later, as an administrator, he continued to press this subject, by, among other things, inviting key speakers to appear before the student body.

Also, LC was a member of the South Sacramento Rotary Club, where I'm confident that he continued to promote his interest in youth, and their necessity of avoiding conflict with the law.

In short, he's a gentleman of the highest order who, for many years, concentrated his efforts behalf of delinquent youth, always urging them not become reinvolved with the law.

Rudy Crew (Sacramento, Tacoma, New York)

With regard to administration, his command of situations was that he wasn't really afraid to stand in his own space and be the person he can be. He exuded confidence and knowledge quite handily.

When I sent him to Luther Burbank High School, I wanted him there for the relationships that he had. He was a guy that basically had followers. He wasn't just a leader with no followers; he had followers. It is the same way as when you have people who go to a church who are disappointed when their pastor didn't preach that Sunday. It was partly because they had followed him when he wasn't a formal leader and they, the people around him, would have been disappointed if he had not been chosen as principal at Burbank.

When I went to New York, I needed him, his toolset, to be a good filter for me. In the industry we are both in, the name of the game is: Can you build a relationship? Can you build relationships with students and the members of the community?

I'm from New York, so I knew this was going to be a heavy lift. I wanted to establish human bona fides - not be some autocrat. I needed somebody to translate those feelings to the outside world and do so authentically. Part of the reasons people bring their own people with them is to provide a filter by someone who knows them and can be candid. Someone to filter-to read the environment from you to them and from them to you.

LC taught me to let things go. I'm a pretty intense person. Things that matter to me, in a value kind of way, when they are not upheld, well, people can be disappointing. I tend to hold on to that too long. LC is so casual. He knows how to hold on to it just long enough to learn from it. He can extract the good from even a bad situation and let the rest go.

Mamie Pinkston (New York City Schools)

A simple "Hello" started our conversation. From our conversation, he appeared to be well diverse and seemingly passionate about his work. I found out that our commonality was that we both worked for the Department of Education; obviously two different departments. We didn't actually work together but since we were both employed by the New York City Department of Education it was pretty interesting.

I remember him talking about the work that he was doing; as I remember, on special assignment. Was working for Rudy (Rudolph) Crew who was the Chancellor. He talked to me about how he, community leaders, and spiritual leaders were working collectively on formulating committees to address the failing school system. I also later found out both he and Chancellor Crew were very passionate about changing the pathology of the failing schools. That was why they reached out to the community and spiritual leaders. Having conversations about the pathology would help improve failing schools.

So, I will say that over a period of time, we remained in communication with each other. Somehow or another he became a mentor. We would call and brainstorm.

I remember how he impacted me personally and professionally with my going back to school; getting my education, He said, "Enjoy what you are doing…it's not going to work."

He helped me with the importance of being a strong role model to my son who was 5 or 6 years old. For me, it was about sitting and reading with my child; fundamentals of education techniques. Education equaled fun. He invited me to attend an all-day workshop in Manhattan with different authors from different genres (children's) who were presenting on the importance of reading with children. Some of the authors even had their own children with them. The beauty of it was that we were able to walk away with signed books. I still have some of them in my library. I was so excited! I came home and sat with him (my son) and read the books. One, it strengthened my relationship with my son; two, it showed me the importance of quality time; and three, he understands that reading IS fundamental.

He's always been a very selfless person; community oriented and family oriented. He believes in a person being self-sufficient. Emotionally, he will lend you a hand and guide you while being professional and compassionate. He has been a mentor, a leader, a resounding voice to me.

I observed he and Chancellor Rudolph Crew working on goals. They achieved getting more family members/parents/grandparents involved in the work. They got the word out to the community leaders on what could be done collectively. It really started opening up the dialogue. Going to the community leaders was the heart of it. Took it into the churches and community and political leaders. I believe their program succeeded in making people realize we are all responsible.

The two magnanimous individuals did everything they could do to create a positive legacy. They met the challenges with plans of action. (They answered)

How can we make it better? Who are the players? Everyone has something in the pot. Their legacy continues to live on. We can go back and look at what programs worked and after they left, who picked up the torch.

At he heart of it, they looked at it from a humanistic point. Always going to be nay-sayers, but they, in my opinion, reached the right people by starting a conversation and it needs to keep going. I was grateful to be a fly on the wall.

Jim Moore (Jackson, MS)

I met LC through a mutual business partner in Jackson, MS. We've been associated for so long, you forget what pulled you together to begin with. We developed software for school training. He helped our company present themselves as Training Resource Associates to the school systems in Sacramento and New York City. He had worked with Rudy Crew; which was beneficial. It was a very data-driven kind of thing. Lots of building-level administrators didn't take to it. Data doesn't let you hide. Because LC is forward-looking, dedicated, and knew how good schools operated, we could convince him of the value. We could tell because of the way his reputation was light years ahead of many school administrators.

Personally, I know he took himself out of Mississippi and positioned himself to become a primal influence in building good educational programs. He is a really special person. It shows in that he got from being black in Mississippi in the 50's to being a first-class educator.

I always looked at LC and thought of him as someone who was not just good and decent; it transcends that. He is a visionary who could see a better way.

He could see in people someone who could fit the vision of what we could do for kids and teachers and administrators. How can it all come back and make it better for parents and become a force greater than itself? That was clear when we first met LC, there was nothing pretentious about him. We could see the depth that he had. Whatever it is, he'd say, "let's deal with it straight-up...let's find a way to overcome in a way to build not tear down". No baby's out with the bathwater with him. He is an old spirit and brings that wisdom with him.

Every one I ever came in contact with about LC thought he could literally walk on water. You- you must be ok because you know LC. LC says you're good - let's get going! LC said you could do it.

Betty, my wife, she says it is no small thing to get involved in your own story. If LC Johnson thought I could contribute to his story, it honors me. That's the way I feel about LC. One word, I hope you have heard this from others, the word is GENUINE.

Val Archer (Tuskegee Airmen)

Of course I didn't know him in the first stage of his life, but later, with Tuskegee Airmen. I think that we're pretty much on the same page with conversations.

LC has been most active with Tuskegee Airmen working with different corporate sectors people in business, government, teachers and young people. Was and is an effective negotiator with and on behalf of kids. He is a good man with finance.

I worked very closely with LC when we specifically were working with Delta Airlines. He has that personality to draw people and get a commitment for projects, especially on behalf of kids.

Boy, do we ever need conversations now in our election process (and results). Our kids in the next few generations are in deep trouble if they don't get good guidance from somewhere. Some schools are better and some worse. Somehow, my generation missed the boat and didn't get the job done in passing on better ideas. I'm still trying - I think I officially/unofficially retired this year. But if more people don't stand up and get involved, people like LC and me, we are stuck with carrying the torch.

Andy Miller (Salvation Army)
LC: I have to interject some clarity here. You see, there is a legacy with the Andy Millers of the Salvation Army and it is only right to remember the first Andy Miller I met years ago along with his grandson.

Lawrenceville Georgia's Salvation Army Captain, Andy Miller III is not the first Andy Miller to serve the Salvation Army in Gwinnett County. His grandfather shared the name that brings to mind thoughts of hard work, commitment to community, and friendship. It was Commissioner Andy Miller who first sought me out for work within the much needed and ever-growing Salvation Army Atlanta's Lawrenceville Corps.

The elder Andy wrote to me in the jacket of his own memoirs, *To a friend, LC, with gratitude. Andy Miller.*

We often spoke about the very topics contained in the elder Miller's memoirs. Small beginnings, destiny, building foundations, Christ-Centered public relations, and models of leadership were among the topics we discussed. He was a great leader and he brought me onto the board where I could do the most good. With the Salvation Army, I was able to use the tools I already had and add some of his-he was a great leader. May he rest peacefully.

Captain Andy Miller, III:

He was friends with my grandfather who was also in Rotary. He was similar to LC and once told LC he would be on SA board. It was unique that my grandfather had an influence on him. I really feel like he is my friend. We can take care of our business pretty quickly and then we talk. I am in my 30's and he is in his early 80's, but I enjoy conversation with him.

He's such an interesting person. I was trying to figure out- as a new Salvation Army Officer- trying to figure out who's on board. You see, we are on an itinerant system, so we need to find out who's who and go to them. It is all in how you associate with people-their finances are irrelevant.

LC was in the military and then education/administration. He came here to Gwinnett from his last service in education from New York. I think of those as being really interesting and large systems. All of his professional talent is not connected to his service-he just came on the scene and began volunteering.

The racial piece is important. He is not going to scare anyone. He has no "black agenda", but he is very aware of who he is. He has managed to become a part of a community. Most influential leaders know him, but he has made himself an influencer by being on these boards. He puts you at ease and then asks guests about themselves. He starts conversations with people all the time.

My first year here at Salvation Army, the board was tough. LC had served for a couple of years as chair. He had the plaque and said, "thanks" - then "retired" out of it. The person I followed in my role here had got pulled early and the board didn't get to vote on a new chair, I had no chair and wasn't sure what to do. I talked to LC a little, but he had just finished up and said he couldn't chair again. Another person volunteered. Things just did not work out as planned. Somehow, she did not fit in with the mission as a whole.

Our Board works as an advisory board and the Board was trying to find its identity. I really thought I was going to lose my Board. I remember a really clear time. I sat down with a mutual friend, Valerie Wages, and LC so I could explain my predicament. LC looked at me and didn't give anything away- he said, "I'm here to support you- I'll step in and be your chair again, I'm here to support your mission."

He can disagree with me, but he tells me, "this is your goal." I think you would have a hard time finding someone to be critical of him. For him, conversation is everything. When he chaired meetings, he would make sure he gave every person a chance to talk. He believes people say things that need to be heard.

LC has had a huge impact on our community. I'm always amazed about what boards he is on. Our Home Sweet Home program began because of 12 Stone Church and the Housing Authority of Gwinnett where he was on the board.

He had his hand on that and made us aware of pretty significant grants. From there, he consulted with us-we are the largest homeless housing provider in Gwinnett.

When he is around the waiting room areas, he goes around to everyone in there and inserts himself into their lives. He makes sure he is connected to all layers of what we do here. He always has his eyes out for people who should come on the board. If he says things, I take them into serious consideration. I really feel like he is a friend. We can take care of our business pretty quickly and then we talk- a 36 year old and an 81 year old.

He serves as the senior African American man in Rotary. I don't know how many African Americans are in Rotary. Our Rotary is dominated by white older men. Even for me, I don't have the money or resources or success like these men do. I can see a big minority. He doesn't just walk through to the boardroom. With him, the tensions and polarities are eased.

Connie Wiggins (Gwinnett Clean and Beautiful)

I remember LC started a conversation with me. He invited me to lunch and said he wanted to volunteer his time to help the community. Gwinnett is blessed by people like LC. These people are why Gwinnett County is so successful and where we are today.

I recruited him to be on the Board of Directors for Gwinnett Clean and Beautiful. He jumped right in with time, great wisdom, and integrity. He rolled up his sleeves and became a great ambassador. He created mini networks promoting our work and why it was important. I wish we had more LC Johnsons.

Absolutely our relationship started with a conversation. That's how he engaged other people in helping us engage others. He understands the art of relationships. I'm always reminded of John Maxwell's saying, "Seek to understand before seeking to be understood." He listens to what is important to people and then engages them with their interests. I have seen him many times turn people who were focused on the problems and get them engaged in seeking a solution.

I can see him in the military. Some people just have a knack for doing this. I can see how that military training and those thinking skills have played a part in how he makes a difference in the community. He is thoughtful and strategic, not manipulative. He gets others to join in and helps people see they can be a part of a solution.

John Edmund Haggai (Peachtree Corners)

About LC, well, number one, unlike so many who are born in Mississippi, of a minority group, he sees himself as an accomplisher, a victor. It never dawns on him that what he says he is going to do will not be accomplished. When I think of him, I think of achievement, accomplishment, and winning. He really is a role model for anyone who wants to become a success. I consider success to be the progressive realization of a God-honoring goal and he fits that description perfectly.

When it comes to conversations, of course his secret is he discusses benefits centering on the listener. He concentrates on the receiver and he gets better results because nobody gets tired of talking about themselves. Nobody changes the conversation when there is a positive conversation going on about themselves.

We met at Peachtree Corners Baptist Church. I always call him General because he was in the military. I don't care what his rank is, but I consider him a general. I assigned to him a term I thought appropriate. It would seem to me that in the military you have to be goal-oriented. If ever there was a man who was goal-oriented, it's that man. Most people have no goals and hit a target every time.

I enjoy watching his body language. 56% of communication, I've been told, comes not from words; his body language is a fascinating study. He is a succeeder, an achiever - amazing. While other people are pondering, he is acting; he moves ahead. Some people get ready to get ready; never get started. At 92 years of age, I can be fairly objective and not worried about anyone taking issue with me. God Bless you LC.

Lynette Howard (Peachtree Corners)
LC's biggest role, when he first moved to Peachtree Corners was to get involved-really involved. He was instrumental in moving the work along to help form Peachtree Corners as a city. He worked hard to get the attendance at United Peachtree Corners Civic Association up for board meetings. He told me, "We have to have fabulous door prizes! Of course Trader Joe's will want to give a door prize."

He is also great at going around the room at meetings looking for newer couples and engaging them in conversation. LC is very cordial and very influential when he speaks to people. I know Peachtree Corners would not have been a city without UPCCA. With LC on the one of the largest HOA boards in Georgia, our city became a reality. He worked hard. LC was always sharing the story and how positive it would be for the community. He talked about forming the city naturally, daily, and all day long-personally networking for it.

He is remarkable. LC has no inhibitions; he rubs his hands together and says, "Hello, it's nice to meet you." Whenever he walks into a place for coffee or lunch, everyone has to come over and say, "Hi!" He knows about them and their kids; who is off to what college- you have to have someone like that when doing campaigns like forming a city.

Personally, I think the best tool in his toolbox is his positive persistence- he is very consistent in being positive. If LC has to get stern about things because there is a problem or something is not going correctly, he has no reservations about stopping and redirecting things.

One of my opponents in a county commission race and I had some difficulty. LC pulled me aside and said, "I don't appreciate the bad things being said on both sides." He really believes in the positive. A lot of us are positive, but for LC, it is a part of his makeup-his health. He always says, "Let's figure it out".

He also doesn't really ever assume that he would fail. You can always see him thinking, "How am I going to get it done a different way if things are not going right?" He is definitely leaving a legacy. I am grateful he picked Peachtree Corners and Gwinnett County. He is a great individual.

One vivid memory I have was when I was a county commissioner during the time Home Sweet Home (A Salvation Army project) came up for funding. There are a lot of different things that go into being a county commissioner and somehow, it got overlooked. LC just called me and said, "Lynnette, I thought you might want to know that funding for HSH was omitted." It was reinstated and LC called me just to say, "Thank you very much."

He neatly gets things done and helps so many people-I don't think they really know what he does for them. He encourages everybody to get involved and tries to seek out minorities so they can be in the right place in leadership roles.

Mike Mason (Peachtree Corners

I asked LC to serve on a committee or board when I need someone who can provide perspective and good judgment when the City (or before that, the UPCCA Board) needed a representative who could be trusted to put the organization's needs first, and not their own personal agenda. LC could have easily run for public office, and been quite successful. Instead, he has helped innumerable elected officials and other leaders with a word of advice or encouragement as well as providing a steadying presence in a critical role.

Phil Wolfe (Hospital system)

Originally, I met LC in 2006 at a Rotary Meeting. I had come from California and I can remember my first impression. I thought he was a quiet, thoughtful, deliberate person-not quick to rush to judgment. And today he remains a reflective and deliberate observer and listener. Part of his worldly experience-he has been a lot of places.

We joke about the military and healthcare as we have moved so frequently it's like we are in the witness protection program. He is certainly easy to talk/chat with and enjoys a great sense of humor. He is an uplifter, not a downer-restores energy-not a drainer. LC is fun to be around.

He does that- starts conversations. I don't know HOW he does it, but he is good at it. I think that's intuitive in people who are good at it- they don't think about it. When it does happen, he can disagree in a very agreeable way. On my board at the hospital, he can be very agreeable in the boardroom. If he disagrees, he always brings things to me in private. He is supportive of the CEO and I like that he comes to talk to us with no hidden agendas. That makes him effective.

I've known him for ten years and I also know his wife Gracie. She has had some physical issues, but I never heard him complain-never wrings his hands like a victim. He just deals with it.
One thing I find remarkable is that he doesn't look or act his age Like his son, Darryl, he has good physical genes. He looks chiseled, handsome and, articulate. I think that about LC - like he has been blessed and takes care of himself.

He is an African American trying to make his way without being offensive. Works on inclusion as much as he can - supports diversity in our ranks, but he also wants to put the right person in the job.

In board meetings, he is not the first to speak - not one to talk, but people don't realize what a critical thinker he is. Good "read" of people. He helps me no matter what I do. Again, I think in traveling around the world, his intuition developed with regard to reading people.

Gwinnett is a much better place because of LC. He is… A Giver, A Doer, A Joiner, A Volunteer… He gets involved, he is not afraid to get involved and stay active. He is not really "retired". He is one of my favorite people and is good for Gwinnett County and good for our hospital. I think he brings a lot to the table and I am glad he's on our team.

Lastly, it is powerful to be around LC - you become a better person- a leader. Selfishly, when I find those kinds of folks, I want to cling to them for the greater good. He shows you can be the best you can be or more.

Bert Nasuti (Gwinnett County)
I met LC in the early 2000's. He had not been here that long. He was a retired educator. I met him at community meetings and then at the Peachtree Corners Community Association. He is a good guy and I really enjoyed talking to him. He was anxious to serve and get involved

When I got elected to the planning commission in 2002, I had some political appointments to make. LC was among the first I tapped. Lots of times people would make appointments and then hover over. That is not my philosophy. My only requirement is that you be a free thinker and make our own decisions.

I got tremendously good feedback. LC was hands-on in the literal meaning. I had 36 political appointees and there is nothing worse than appointing someone and getting a call to replace. When it comes to a meeting that matters - he is there. I consider him the consummate involved citizen. He is smart and well liked. He has chosen to give back to the community over and over again. He has certainly had an influence in making this county a better place. I am glad he is around

Beauty Baldwin (Boy Scouts)

I say that LC is a community activist. That's how I label him. He and I are involved in a lot of different things together; NE GA Council - Boy Scouts, Rotary...several boards. He is also one of the persons that I chose when we decided to do a charter school unique to GA - Fine Arts and Academics. I needed someone with administration in education background. LC has been an active member of the board and is always doing anything you need from a board member, he's just that kind of person.

I am the Vice President of the Cultural Diversity Committee for the North East Georgia Council for the Boy Scouts of America. L.C. is an active member of my committee whom I depend on for his expertise and experience. We are charged to get minority boys engaged in scouting. We are very interested in providing means for disadvantage boys to become involved with scouting. We explore ways to get parents of these young boys interested in seeing the importance of scouting and how it can benefit their child.

LC knows a lot of people in the community and people trust him. That has been a big plus. They know when we are begging them it's for a good thing. Scouting is such an asset growing up for boys. Keeps them busy and LC believes in keeping kids busy in a positive manner.

The reason we are on this earth is to serve. I love to see people giving and he knows how to serve. He is so well-known anywhere you go. You think about LC, how much he contributes. He is a community activist. This is so important at this time in his life. He believes that if you want anything to happen, you get involved in your community. If you are a servant-leader yourself, it is easier to get others involved. Young people would like to be like that - like LC.

Jim Maughan (Scouts and Rotary)

He and I were in Rotary together. We became good friends and started sitting together every Tuesday. Our wives were good friends too. My wife really took on to Gracie. Since my wife had a stroke, we don't have that contact we had due to illness, but we had good times.

From the beginning, LC was easy to talk to and I believe I actually asked him to become a board member for the Northeast Georgia Boy Scouts. I became president about 2-3 years ago and since I was president, I asked him to be Vice President of Administration and he did.

One of our goals was to get more African American, Hispanic, and underprivileged boys involved. We had lots of contacts and added 6-8 new African American board members to the Executive Board of Northeast Georgia Council. Prior to this effort, there were just 2-3 in Athens and one in Gainesville. We expanded it and got Beauty Baldwin re-involved with groups that got African American kids more involved in Scouting. She and LC had a very good blend of Scouting, leadership skills, and good growth skills.

He and I, we've talked quite a bit over the phone and we still conversate along with Beauty and Alvin Wilbanks (Gwinnett County Schools Superintendent) who were very involved in helping us with this- getting African American staff members and making progress in our schools.

When I was president, we went to Camp Rainey Mountain together and met with many troops from other states. It just so happened that there was a scout troop from Flora, MS/Madison County area. We went and visited with the scoutmaster. I remember that LC was just so excited to see that. Brought tears to his eyes to know that things had changed in his hometown.

In order to have change, you've got to get the parents. We are trying to figure out how to reach out to parents. We got the kids involved, but we have to figure out how to get the parents involved. It's not as fast as I would like to see it. LC sees that positive steps are making progress. He is not only a booster, but a worker in all that. He is solid. He is one of my best friends. He is not going let you down. He says he's going do something; he does it. I guess that's why we get along so well - we are both doers. He is always talking about the next steps.

Wayne Sikes (Rotary & Hospital Board)

I think we met at Rotary. You know how it is with people you feel you have known forever. I don't know a time when I didn't know LC. As long as I have known him, he has been an even-tempered person who always remains above the fray.

LC has been around and has experienced a lot. I think it is why he stays so calm. At one time, how can I be delicate about this? Well, I won't. We didn't have a lot of black people in our Rotary, which is a problem. When I was chairman of the Hospital Board of Directors, I was very much aware of our lack of diversity in both color and gender. Diversity is so important when you represent a community; you have to represent everybody. At the time, we had no African Americans on the Board. I had been on the lookout for someone who was not a token. We needed a contributing, functioning person. We had some representation among Asian and Indian cultures and some women, but not anyone like LC. I sort of made it my mission to bring him on board.

LC and I have talked about the representation problems in Gwinnett County. We don't have a diverse representation that matches our population. Asking LC, a well-spoken, intelligent person to serve on the Board struck me as a good idea. He had a track record of bringing a good perspective from his constituency.

LC would make the Board aware of issues and is always willing to participate in discussion that is good for the whole. Early on, I said I wanted him to be involved in recruiting. There is no one more objective to bring these diversity issues to the table. Besides that, LC is a great friend and a nice guy who is an asset to our community.

David McClesky (Hospital Board)

LC's current situation is a testament to his upbringing. We are a good community and getting better. We have bridged challenges with our own diversity. Our diversity is strength in our community and LC has been an asset.

This is where we live, work, and play as well as learn and be healthy within our school districts, hospitals, and secondary education facilities. We have a medical college here. We have a richness of doctors and a legacy in Gwinnett. Our physician workforce in Gwinnett is a significant contribution.

Like LC, I am an educator. I began in 1976 as a teacher in the Gwinnett School District. God has blessed me and I am fortunate to be of service. As a fellow servant-leader, I see LC's leadership as multidimensional. There are basically three fronts. One, the man is committed to improving the greater Gwinnett community as a whole for the good of all. He is engaged vs. involved. He sees things bloom. He has the tenacity to stick to his commitments and see them through to completion.

Second, he is inspirational by using talents and skills accumulated through years. He sees the talent in each individual and models talent. His work at the hospital has been valued on all fronts. In the community and with assignments, he notes the benefit barometer the hospital has had. There is nobody who advocates as smoothly as LC.

Third, he is engaged. When LC is engaged with you, he has ideas of where to bring in talent from diverse backgrounds. He believes, "I'll champion this for these reasons…" He is better connected than AT&T.

Gracie is his champion. Our spouses are friends. Gracie has been right with him and knows the struggles he has had as an African American growing up in tough times. What it was like to be model citizens because of who they are. She is a cornerstone.

You can always count on our Board of Trustees. LC is there early and stays late. He tours every room during an opening, engaging with every person. He represents the hospital with fidelity.

He's an artist with conversations. He provides the canvas and the people he engages with fill the canvases with the colors of their strengths. He helps people realize the strengths and also improvements. He artistically develops them into leaders.

As a Southern Baptist, I see him as a fine example of humble leadership and servitude. We have all benefitted from all the boards he has served on. He has never left a place without making it better. LC is dynamic, humble, and tenacious; he brings things to closure. I am honored to serve with him.

Drew Serrero (Student, Composer, Friend)

I have had an opportunity to watch this memoir grow from a conversation to reality and have read every word more than once while it was in the editing stages. The real reason I got to read it before all of you was that I was asked by the co-writer (my mother) to create a musical theme for the video series that will accompany this book. Since music is what I do best, I was honored.

I was even more honored to meet with Mr. Johnson and have some real conversations with him. During those conversations, and while I read the words he has offered to you in this memoir, one thing seemed to be missing. That one thing was hope. It saddens me that our world isn't what Mr. Johnson thought it would be by now. And by now, I mean my time. My time is a time for youth to take notice of our world and how we can commit to doing the most good.

Just like Mr. Johnson was influenced by his teacher, Mr. McMillian, and the boy with the blue Air Force jacket, I am influenced by people like LC Johnson and my own teachers. I want to do the most good, which is why I plan to go into music education. While teaching school has become very difficult, I am encouraged to know that I can build my own toolbox full of great advice to help me achieve my goals. Proper introductions, good conversation with plenty of room for listening, and keeping my own moral compass pointed true will all be placed into my toolbox as I head off to college.

Unlike many kids, I grew up in a multi-generational household. I had the advantage of parents and grandparents who are unwavering in their support of the dreams of their children and grandchildren. They don't judge, they just show up to chaperon, sell concessions, cheer from the stands, and hold conversations with anyone and everyone. They are good role models, just like Mr. Johnson.

So, what I am really telling the readers is to hold out hope. The future is not bleak. My own tribe is a culmination of all students with whom I have grown up that come in many colors, shapes, sizes, temperaments, religions, and beliefs. What we have in common is the language of music that allows us to "conversate" on more than one level. People love music of all types and that helps us to all come together without regard to our differences.

What I plan to do for the future is teach music to a whole new generation so that they too can go out into the world, hold conversations, fill their toolboxes with effective tools, and do the most good.

Gracie's Story

Editor's Note: She was born Gracie Mae Rogers in Jackson, Mississippi. For most of her thirty-five year teaching career, Gracie Johnson taught first graders to read and write in mostly black schools until she met and married LC in 1968. Together, with her daughter from her first marriage, Valerie, Gracie and LC embarked on the military life. In 1970, their son, Daryl, was born. Eventually, the family ended up in California where classrooms looked a little more racially balanced and the weather was more than agreeable. Gracie taught school, LC finished up his military career and looked towards a new chapter. Little did he know, at the suggestion of his schoolteacher wife, he would end up in education. Gracie's many years in the classroom, with coveted summers off, had an effect on the military man she had married.

I didn't know it when we met, but we did make a difference in children's lives. They are so eager and want to learn. They come to you not knowing their letters, they can't read yet, and by the end of the year, they can read. It makes you feel so good inside. It always made me feel good to have parents ask for me-for their kids to be in my classroom. In California, it was both black and white families-what a difference.

I did encourage him to get into education.

I met LC through a cousin of mine after I finished college. We didn't have that much in common. He was in the service and I was a teacher with a young daughter. He thought I talked too much and wondered "who in the world is this person." I guess it grew on us. We got married in Jackson at the Justice of the Peace because there was never enough time. I figured I would travel with him, but I never left the states. I did get to see a lot of the states though.

When it came to Daryl, you see Valerie was almost on her own by the time we got to California, we wanted him to be introduced to a better part of life than we had growing up. We wanted to give him the opportunity to do what he wanted and that is exactly what he is doing. He is an actor in California now and he seems happy. My older daughter, Valerie lives in Sacramento and works for the San Juan School District.

I guess we taught Daryl to give back too. He makes time to read to students. He loves kids.

I've always been next to LC. After I retired from school teaching in 1994, I supported what he was doing. I don't complain when he is gone. It is a "habit of life" for us. I always wanted him to feel free to do what he has to do. He knows I'm here if he needs me.

When it came to education, well, I guess in life too, we both believe in giving everyone a chance-everyone. Whether they were privileged or underprivileged, there is good in everyone, you just have to find it. Sometimes, it's hard, but it pays off to find the good in people. He takes a chance on most people, especially the underprivileged.

Church has always been important to us. In the service, we used the base chapel. We always find a church where we felt we could do good. We were raised/brought up in the church which is a good thing. I'm not really an outgoing person like LC. I don't start something, but if someone needs me to do something, I'll do it. But mostly, I am a bench member who helps out in any place I can. It comes easier with children for me. I listen. I was known to be talkative in my younger life, but now, I wait and turn in it over in my mind as to what's best to do.

After I retired, I did like to stay home, but if LC had an event for the school system, I would go. It was my way of supporting him. When we lived on Long Island, I would attend the entertainment events in LC's district.

We moved to Georgia in 1998 from New York. When we moved here, our address was Duluth and none of this growth was here. The big city came to us. Now, our city is named Peachtree Corners. LC was a part of that.

We are a Golden Rule Family. Treat everybody the way you would like to be treated. LC's a dedicated person and whatever he gets in, he wants to work it out to the end. It's like my knee replacement, he keeps pushing me. He's a nagger for the good. He brings out the best in everybody he meets. I hope the world will see LC through this book.

Daryl's Words

Let me tell you about my dad…

Not only has he been a tremendous father, a mentor, a role model, a hero, and one of my best friends throughout my life, he, along with my mom, have blessed me with the social characteristics and mental tools to have a competitive edge with life challenges.

I was born on an Air Force military base in Altus, Oklahoma to LC Johnson and Gracie Johnson. Shortly after being born, my dad was sent to Vietnam. The health of my Grandpa on my mom's side was deteriorating, so we relocated to Jackson, MS to take care of him. This was where my parents were raised so we were surrounded by family from both sides. My mom had 9 brothers and a sister and several kinfolks living locally on my dad's side; both grandparents and close relatives.

My dad returned later that year, after my Grandpa passed and we moved to Texas. We were in Texas for about a year before my dad was transferred to Mather Air Force Base in Sacramento, CA. We lived on base, and I remember my dad in uniform. Leaving early for his daily duties on base, coming home in the afternoon, scooping me up and driving off in the truck. We would stop off at the bait shop for either worms or fish eggs and then go fishing for the afternoon.

Often, we would grab a hotdog and soda from this tiny spot on base, then we would sit on the bank of a river, lake, or bridge and cast out 2 lines. My dad was an avid fisherman and was very enthusiastic. He was often discovering new spots from his network of fishing buddies. Dad had been fishing since he was a kid, so he knew all the nuances of fishing and was a very patient and quiet man. I was often so excited to be with my dad that I would throw rocks into the water and make loud noises. My dad would put his hand on my shoulder and say, "Son, you're going to scare away all the fish because you're making too much noise...relax son!" I was apologetic, but confused because I didn't think the fish had ears. We took many fishing trips and developed a cool bond during those early years. The peace and energy of fishing by the water is something I still maintain today...and ironically, I don't eat fish!

Growing up on a military base was very inclusive. They was no reason to leave because everything was provided for. Groceries at the commissary, toys at the BX, bowling alley, barbershop, preschool, etc… This gave a special meaning to the fishing trip excursions that my dad and I would take. I saw a lot of exciting military equipment and shows such as the Thunderbirds and Blue Angels. I was a true military brat and still, to this day, support and applaud the services that the military provides for this country!

Things changed when my dad retired from the military and we moved to a middle class suburban area called Orangevale, CA. That is where I was raised in what I know as my first home with a front and back yard and my own room. My transition from military life to suburban life was impactful in many ways. One, there were (was) no more black people. I started kindergarten at Twin Lakes Elementary School. It was predominantly an all-white school and was very intimidating in the beginning. I was young, but I remember that feeling of comfort knowing school monitors during lunch and recess. His job duties included making sure that the kids "played nice" during the breaks and at lunch. He, however, always seemed to be close whenever any type of confrontation or mischief occurred where I was playing. Like a Superhero, he would appear and say, "Daryl, are you ok?"

Dad and Mom had a major influence on my childhood and, as an African American, I realize how blessed I was to have both my parents in my life from birth. At a young age, they made it clear to me that my abilities to achieve were based on what I made of it. Color of skno was no excuse and only meant I needed to overachiever for equal value in life.

My dad and I became involved in Indian Guides and, later, Boy Scouts. These organizations had an amazing impact on our Father/Son quality time. Weekly activities and projects for us to work on together with other father and son's in the troop. We developed projects within the community, engaged in philanthropy, and organized fishing and camping trips.

Yes! More fishing! Staying involved within the community is something my dad is always a strong advocate of. One of his constant mantras has been, "Get Involved Son!" He, to this day, remains involved in several organizations, committees, boards and advisories.

I developed a hunger for reading and writing. I was cast as the head in a school theatrical play. I was the narrator in a school play and that was when I discovered the power of the spoken word and the effectiveness of vocabulary and its communication on people. My parents encouraged my reading enthusiasm by enrolling me in book clubs and getting my first library card.

The folks kept me occupied with many after school activities, clubs, and organizations within the community. There was always something to do and very little time to be idle. Dad planted seeds of strong self-esteem and commitment to being efficient and independent. My dad would say, "Whatever you do in life son, strive to be the best you can be at doing it, even if you're going to be a garbage collector." Jokingly, he would say it, but he meant every word. It still lingers in my ears today giving me motivation and work ethic.

As I was being groomed to become a man, I was introduced to my first sport, "soccer". I played in the house, at school, in the street, wherever there was a small ball to kick. I was exceptionally fast as a kid and at the age of 6, my parents signed me up to play organized soccer on a team called the Strikers. From that day on, my parents never missed one of my games. We would travel to tournaments and games on the weekend with other families with a boy on the team. I excelled at this sport and was praised by many coaches as I got better.

My favorite coach was my dad who would imitate other players and tell me how to be more aggressive on the field as a metaphor with life. "Son, you can't be timid. Go out there and take the ball." Soccer became the family thing. I, later, would try out for a club team and then it was 100% commitment. The thing that resonates with me the most was that, at any game, in any city, I could always look over to the sideline and know that my dad and mom were there and always had my back.

My turn to talk about some people...
Again, it is exceptionally humbling to read the words that people have said about me. I've been to a few awards ceremonies in my time and many times listened to a list of accomplishments, but reading what others have actually taken the time to SAY about me is a whole other ballgame.

One thing I picked up on right away was the ease with which my friends of different cultures were willing to talk about diversity. Living in a county like Gwinnett, it is discouraging and yet, fascinating that we have so little diversity in our representation in government, education, and boards of directors. I would really have thought by now we would have come much farther than we have.

While I have seen a lot in my time here on this earth, I can't say I have any real good answer for why diversity should have to still be a "thing" as the young folks like to say. I wouldn't be honest if I didn't say I am a little disappointed in the powers that be on all sides of the issue.

Sometimes, people continue to serve in roles long beyond their desire or effectiveness because, well, nobody else will do it. Sometimes, people are afraid to step forward and others are afraid to push anyone who isn't just like them. I think fear of starting some sort of race war (or skirmish) keeps people from reaching out and talking about the real issues at hand. I think, people should stop being so sensitive and just talk it out. We need to heal the rifts, not cause more because we don't take the time to look at things through the eyes of others.

And we have issues. Several of my friends have made note that a cotton farmer from Mississippi during the rumblings of the civil rights movements did well to get out of THE SOUTH and into the Air Force. I have to agree. I didn't want to farm cotton for my whole life-that's for sure. But the issues that were rumbling back then, seem to still be rumbling now. I know what it is like to have folks talk about you like you are some sort of Uncle Tom, but the reality is, if we don't challenge that sort of thinking and the "powers that be" don't reach out, we will never get any further than we are today which is nowhere near far enough in my opinion.

Divisions and negativity are a waste of energy. If only people on all sides of an argument would realize that we would get something done. If we were to collaborate as a whole people, a unit, like my days in the Air Force, we would have more significant negotiations. I think back to Florin Road, to all those car dealerships who had those signs that began with "No Burbank Students Allowed" all over the place. Negativity like that breeds more negativity. With that kind of division, nothing will ever get done. People have to stop thinking that if they compromise they have lost. We have to see compromise for what it really is; a meeting of the minds, not a loss.

Take my good friend Beth for example; she is helping me write up these words. Where do you think we would be if I saw her as too white to write in my voice? Nowhere at all. I had to reach out to her and she to me in order for this process of creating a book to come to fruition. She has ideas and so do I, but at the end of the day, she has listened to my words and interviewed my friends to paint a pretty good word picture of who I am. And who I am is LC Johnson, Still A Soldier.

Friends MVT: Always know who you are and look for a reflection of yourself in those around you.

Chapter 9
The Importance of Awards, Accolades, and Breaking Bread

Do not withhold good from those to whom it is due, when it is in your power to do it. Proverbs 3:27

Service without recognition is a concept that I just cannot wrap my head around. I have enjoyed several tangible awards and accolades in my eighty-plus years, but they are nothing close to the intrinsic reward I feel when a job is well done. I know that when I am promoted to heaven, it will not be on the works that I have done, but on the walk that I have made as a believer. But works, because they have their place and are so necessary to our humankind as a whole, must be rewarded or the likelihood of people participating in doing good may be diminished.

Again, it is simple psychology. Read some B.F. Skinner if you have any questions on reward systems. Basically, if someone does something, and that behavior is rewarded, the chance of that person continuing to do that same thing is more likely, or reinforced, if you like. It is the pretty much the same with awards. If the board of directors of a certain company or organization would like to encourage the volunteers or employees of that company or organization to do a good job, well then, they need to provide some reward.

Over the years, I have been to a few awards ceremonies. Some awards are small, like the ribbon a student might get for being the best weekly speller in their classroom. I can remember the classic gold star as if it were yesterday. A little gold foil star when placed at the top of a graded paper was as good as real gold back in my days at school.

I have to say that a little foil gold star was probably among the most important first rewards in the lives of many kids. I was reminded of just such feelings upon receiving a bronze medal from the United State Air Force for meritorious service. Even though I was an adult with a family and a long career behind me, it still felt really great to be rewarded for a job well done.

Maybe my fascination with education began in the early days of reading to orphans in Korea, or maybe it was Mr. McMillian, my high school math teacher. Maybe it was a combination of things, but one thing is for certain, I am dedicated to education in as many forms as it may take. I guess that is why I think rewarding students, teachers, and all the support staff has to take place at various times. Some work harder than others and that should be reflected, but the simple "atta-boy or atta-girl" is one of those things that should be considered a part of anyone's vocabulary.

During the time I served as an educator in Sacramento, Tacoma, and New York, I collected a number of "gold stars" that took many different forms. I think, the most important form was the simple thank you note.

In this day and age of everything electronic- I mean you can Google anything you need to know in an instant or two- the simple act of putting pen to paper seems to have gotten lost. It is that way with news as well. The news seems to be more inciting than informative and lacks the local flavor that defined local newspapers from the very start. But back in the day, newspapers helped me establish a different narrative for the students and neighborhood surrounding

Luther Burbank High School. From those changes came awards, accolades and, the blessed handwritten note pointing out the joy others took from the work I was administering with the help of all of those around me.

Of Note:

Some of the messages I received described the changes - positive changes - we were making to the schools I administered. Back at California Middle School, people like Principal, George Robertson wrote:

I would like to take this opportunity to commend you for the excellent opening of the 1985-86 school year…Our partnership in this endeavor promises to be exciting as we meet the challenges of our ever changing educational system.

His comments came on the heels of my tenure as a long-term substitute for one of the vice principals. There was so much going on during that time and my attentions were directed at doing the best job such that I didn't really stop to think about whether I would be recognized for my efforts. His notes that ended up in my personnel file helped me to find my place at Luther Burbank some years later.

Louise A. Perez, President of the Sacramento Unified School District Board of Education once wrote to me:

…Thank you for all of your time and energy in chairing this worthwhile activity for our middle school students.

Her comments were more than worthy since it helped teach me that chairing an event or a committee shouldn't be a struggle. It is much more of a reward and it is nice to be recognized for the efforts.

Now, as it happened, I ended up as principal during a teacher strike. I won't revisit that so much as to say that because of our efforts as administrators, our expertise was later called upon to shepherd another school district through a similar situation. In a letter addressed to Superintendent, Dr. Rudy Crew in 1989, The Grant Joint Union High School District thanked us profusely for providing materials and information to weather the storm of a teacher strike and still manage instruction. Their acknowledgement was appreciated and shows how districts need to work together for the highest good of all students, educators, and staff.

So you get that my education career benefitted greatly from some very well placed notes of gratitude. I want to take a little space to document some civic expressions of thanks.

I cannot say enough about my friend, Fred Teichert whose foundation stirred the various local powers to come together for the benefit of the community through the Boys and Girls Clubs of Greater Sacramento. We met, of course, through a conversation about my needs at Luther Burbank High School and that extended into a "you scratch my back, I'll scratch yours" relationship. What I mean is, I lent my expertise to his board of directors and he helped me get the things we needed for the school. In all, it was the kids of the community who most benefitted from our many meetings over coffee (there it is again) and lunch or dinner. Whatever the meeting, breaking bread together, and with others, led to the best outcomes possible.

Awards...that little something for your shelf

Gracie and I do love a good baseball game. We were thrilled to learn that our own county would have a minor league ballpark that would be host to the farm team, The Gwinnett Braves. Fast forward a bit to July of 2010 where I found myself honored to be the "10th Man" at a Christmas in July celebration and food drive for The Salvation Army. Because I was serving as the Gwinnett Advisory Board Chair, the G-Braves threw in an award reserved for persons who "Best Embody the Spirit of Gwinnett". I have to say, it was an honor and I completely enjoyed my day along with many members of our facility and the Rotarians I press into service each Christmas season to ring bells on behalf of The Salvation Army. So, you see, an award like that belongs to all of those who help me do the most good for Gwinnett.

Speaking of Rotarians, I am blessed to share my current Rotary Club with some exemplary people who move and shake about the area. As a past Paul Harris Fellow and a Will Watt Fellow recipient, I am beholden to the men and women of Rotary who helped make both of those awards, which represent a giving spirit, possible.

I think it is most important to consider our government officials. Not only do they provide letters of appreciation to me, but I feel it important to let them know we appreciate their efforts. Pay is certainly not the motivation for most government officials I know. It is a sense of duty to the community. Representation is both a cost and a reward. Anyway, that's how I see it. Take a minute to look up who represents you and drop them a line.

In the news...

Like I was saying earlier in this chapter, you have to have some good news for the people. Matthew, Mark, Luke, AND John said it, so it must be important to proclaim good news. That's why I lament the death of a good old local newspaper. The Internet does have its place, but there is something about printed paper...the feel, the smell, the look, and the concreteness of it all that says that what is on the pages is important.

Over the years, the newspaper has reported the good about things I have done. Whether it was banning lockers at Luther Burbank or flying to Washington, DC with The Tuskegee Airmen, newspapers have covered some amazing moments that I like to remember in print. (Although, as my website develops...you will find some links or documents showing some of these articles...so onward and upward with technology!)

Some of my favorite print news showcased the shakeup I created at Luther Burbank High School. First, there were the lockers-they had to go! They only created a place for students to congregate and get into trouble. I had a bit of pushback at first, but, as the days went on, nobody missed them much; except maybe those who hid things there in the first place.

Second, the return of calm to Burbank made the papers and I even enjoyed one of those handwritten notes from my State Farm agent, Dick Carter, who put a clipping in the envelope as well when he thanked me for the "hard, effective work."

The Salvation Army has been a source of many articles that bring accolades to the efforts of an amazing group of human beings. Providing for the basic, fundamental needs of a community creates a stable environment for all residents.

Another group that I helped establish here in Gwinnett, Peachtree Corners to be specific, is my fraternity, Alpha Kappa Alpha, Psi Omega Omega Chapter. As a thank you for my efforts on their behalf, they honored me with a community service award in 2014 and a scholarship was given at Norcross High School on my behalf in 2015.

While it is very nice to be awarded and have people write and say nice things about, and to you, it is also very satisfying to find yourself among your current neighbors while breaking bread and celebrating achievement. Most recently, I found myself the recipient of an award that meant a great deal to me.

The Paul Duke Lifetime Achievement Award, which recognizes an individual who has generously give of their time, energy, and efforts to improve the quality of life in Peachtree Corners over numerous years, has become one of the most cherished of the awards I have ever received. You see, Paul Duke was a visionary, a guy who first came to Gwinnett County with the idea that people, like him, should have a place where they could also work and place in close proximity to where they lived. The area he chose for his planned development eventually became what is known as Technology Park in Norcross. He pulled in big-name developers who built neighborhoods, established churches, schools, and our local YMCA. He believed that a community needed all of these things to become a good place to live.

From all accounts I have read or heard, he went about things by doing the most good and he did it by starting conversations with people. Obviously, these are qualities that are near and dear to my heart. And because those qualities are so dear to me, it was quite an honor to be presented with the Paul Duke Lifetime Achievement Award on my 81st birthday on October 24th, 2016. It was a fine birthday.

Breaking Bread...and sometimes some not so savory dishes

Rewards feed self-esteem. Because people cannot be expected to run on self-esteem alone, you need to break some bread together. Now, keep in mind, I have lived all over the world and when I say I am not really an adventurous eater, I mean, I am not an adventurous eater. I guess it was being brought up on a southern, home-style, farm-fresh, Baptist buffet that placed me square in the middle of meat and potatoes territory. Regardless of what is placed before me, I am more than likely going to eat it, or at least make a show of pushing things around to make it look like I was maybe not hungry. Again, as an octogenarian, I can blame it on age if I don't eat my whole dinner.

All that being said, I have had the opportunity to share some fine meals with some outstanding company. Conversations over food just seem to come naturally. The food, presentation, and accompaniments are great conversation starters. Sharing a meal is one of my favorite ways to celebrate the accomplishments of those with whom I have served in a variety of capacities over the years. Breaking bread with those around you nourishes the body and the soul.

MVT: Awards, Accolades, and Breaking Bread are all exceptionally important tools for establishing, maintaining, and growing a good organization.

Chapter 10
Legacy Tour of Duty
Advice for current and future soldiers:
Never underestimate the power of a good
conversation.

*"But as for you, son of man, your fellow citizens who talk about you
by the walls and in the doorways of the houses, speak to one
another, each to his brother, saying, 'Come now and hear what the
message is which comes forth from the LORD.' Ezekiel 33:30*

*Let your speech always be with grace, as though seasoned with salt,
so that you will know how you should respond to each person.
Colossians 4:6*

*And what you have heard from me in the presence of many
witnesses entrust to faithful men who will be able to teach others
also. Timothy 2:2*

The most likely picture anyone might conjure up when considering "the last
men out" of the Vietnam war zone would probably encompass some sort of
frontline soldier carrying an AK under one arm and maybe a wounded buddy
under the other all while running from a huge orange explosion in the jungle.
In the end, and I do mean the very end, that's not how it was at all. Strangely
enough, the very last military personnel to leave were crisply dressed, carried
briefcases, and walked calmly to an awaiting Lockheed C-141 Starlifter.

The real point to this analogy is that once the frontline fighting is done, there
is still diplomacy, mountains of paperwork, and plenty of property to

disperse. It takes all manner of personnel to win any battle. Whether you are fighting for freedom, rights, property, life, liberty, the pursuit of happiness or anything worth having, you have to go about it in the most non-divisive manner possible. Supporting our front lines in the supply chain was what I did best; so, that's how I ended up as one of the last out of Vietnam. You might say, I had the closing shift.

Leaving Vietnam took a great deal of diplomacy and plenty of conversation. You know, basic communication skills. Running a supply chain; getting what one unit needs without shorting another takes diplomacy or you will have a mess on your hands. Lots of situations get messy if you don't take the time to be at least somewhat diplomatic.

Take the hotly contested 2016 presidential election. That was a mess from the get-go, but our form of government allows for voices to be heard, opinions to be tolerated, and debates to ensue. In short, we are allowed to have conversations. Without all this freedom, our country would not be what it is today. Take it or leave it. Without all this freedom, we wouldn't have this outstanding opportunity that spreads out before us to heal all the wounds, perceived or real, which divide us. It begins with a good introduction that leads to conversations and is insured by the blood spilled by countless soldiers on the front lines.

It's time to struggle up and out of toddlerhood and take a stand as grownups who should completely understand you don't always get what you want, the way you want it, when you want it. It just doesn't happen like that. I think it is time for everyone to reach deep into their pockets and pull out their moral compass. Everyone should have one. It may not be fully developed, but it probably resembles the compass provided to me by my parents in Flora, MS so many years ago. For that matter, most people have one; it just might not point in the same direction as some other person's moral compass.

The thing about a moral compass is that it is not tangible in nature. You cannot really hold it in your hands. It is a thing of our own imaginations and imagination can make anything be what we want it to be. In my case, my moral compass was forever evolving the older I got and with the experiences I enjoyed (or endured).

In the end, my moral compass has become the best tool in my toolbox. The needle points straight and true towards a power higher than myself by which I can set my course in life. It reminds me that I am a servant leader and keeps me in check by helping me to remember a time when I was not the type of person who was worthy of the title.

Servant Leaders

While I didn't realize it at the time, my time in Flora allowed me to dabble in leadership. I wasn't necessarily a servant leader. I did serve those who needed me, but it was mostly in response to my mom or dad's request to take so-and-so to the doctor or run a meal by the home of someone in need.

When it came to the farm, I did manage to make a good name for myself with regard to the cotton gin owners. I got black folks to work with white folks and all the cotton made it from seed to sale with a little help from me, and those like me, who could bridge the culture gap with conversational skills.

You see, being able to ask a few questions and then sit back waiting for the answers to reveal themselves is a dying skill. Basic conversation, listening, solving problems in such a way that everyone benefits, without keeping some manner of score, is essential.

Citizenship and Ownership-The Essentials

Some other essentials for a successful legacy are based on belonging. I am talking about ownership and having a sense of citizenship. In my opinion, the population that makes up communities must have some form of both. People who don't feel they belong and lack something tangible that ties them to a place are less likely to participate in the betterment of where they live.

Now, I am not talking about people who might move from one place to another for work or family. If that were the case, I would be considered to be without a sense of ownership. What I am talking about is being deeply rooted and connected no matter where you happen to put your head at night. For example, Gracie and I chose to live in metro Atlanta for a number of reasons. Just because we were strangers to the area was no reason to feel we didn't belong. We made a home, we met some people, we found a place to worship that made us comfortable, and we brought with us our sense of citizenship. The way we established ourselves here was really no different than the way we had established ourselves in any other place we had moved to over the years.

Now, at our age and retirement, we were able to buy a nice home in a nice neighborhood surrounded by a diverse group of very nice people. Not all "ownership" is about owning a house. Ownership, at least in my mind, means that a population has to feel connected to something. Take kids for example. They spend much of their day inside a school building. Whether they are a

Patriot, a Ram, or a Knight, there is a certain amount of "ownership" of the institution they call school. It gives them a sense of belonging. And by "owning" something, they are more likely to be called to be good citizens of the community where they live.

My opinion of citizenship stems from the idea that we are all citizens of one great country that just happens to be located in a universe so vast and so full of potential that every inhabitant must do their very best to do the most good. See what I am getting at? Citizenship is a sort of belonging to something.

In order to be a good citizen, a person has to begin with himself or herself. You have to be able to live with the person staring back at you in the mirror and think that person has some sort of worth. It goes back to self-esteem and our need to have some sort of gratification from others, but also to be able to recognize self-worth. Self-awareness is also essential. I said it in my dissertation, I saw it in juvenile hall, and I felt it to be true during my time in the Air Force. Knowing oneself and believing in the possibilities is important.

Since we have established a body has to be self-aware to be a good citizen, we can move on to what a person can do to be a productive part of our society. For me, joining things, being a part of a greater good or a whole community is absolutely the best way to be a good citizen.

I remember, as a child, saying the Pledge of Allegiance to our flag, to our United States of America. And as a child, I memorized the words and repeated them along with my classmates in a sort of elementary training for the beginnings of great citizenship. But, and I am here to tell each child, teenager, and adult that you cannot know what a privilege it is to be a citizen of The United States of America until you have seen the poverty, hunger and pain in the faces of war orphans. I will tell you outright, if you don't like your circumstances, you are in the best country in the world for realigning your own stars.

Changing your stars begins with taking a step forward. In my case, it began with a bus ride to Jackson, MS where I joined The United States Air Force. Because I joined the Air Force, I was able to work on my higher education. Because I was well educated, I was able to start a second career, or tour of duty in public education. Because I had a career in public education, I leaned how vital it is to be represented at the civic, social, and government levels. All this from a kid who was born on a cotton farm in Southern Mississippi in the 1930's.

I am absolutely not knocking my upbringing or my birthplace. Both gave me a moral compass that has guided me through some interesting times and places. It is just that, as circumstances had it, being a young man of color in the rural South in the 1950's was not the best place for me to further my own life. The military offered me an outstanding place to serve my country, express my citizenship, earn a living, support a family, further my education, and ultimately, continue soldiering on to do the most good.

This chapter is my commentary on the current state of things. I have to say, I wouldn't be an honest man if I didn't express at least some disappointment. Looking back to the 1950's and knowing what I know about life, I thought we would be a better "mixed tribe" by now.

My own personal tribe is richly mixed with people from all cultures. I thought we would have better representation in civic, social, and government matters. We don't. But, I think, because I talk to all sorts of people, each side is still afraid to reach out and mix it up a little. People tend to think that in giving of themselves, they lose something. The opposite is actually truer. It is in giving that we receive.

In this section, and in the soon-to-be-released accompanying video series, I offer a bit of advice from a guy who has been around for a long while and seen a lot of things. Mix your tribe up. Get involved in your community. Be a good citizen. Find a way to have ownership. Google your senators, representatives, and council members. That Google is amazing, you can learn so much and connect with all the right people in order to express your opinion.

Now, don't go expressing your opinions unless you are willing to work, to become involved, for the way you would like to see things done. Your representatives are humans just like you and deserve to be a part of your mixed tribe. Those who work to represent a constituency are not your adversaries just because they might look or act differently. They are there to hold all manner of conversations meant to bring about what is best for the community as a whole.

So, introduce yourself and hold some meaningful conversations. I promise, conversations are the single strongest and most effective tool I have ever placed in my toolbox. I suggest everyone find room for a good conversation in their own personal toolbox. In my opinion, a lifetime of meaningful conversations that touch the lives of others in a positive manner is an outstanding legacy.

Conversations have been my tool of choice throughout all four of the "tours of duty" that have defined my life. Whether I was serving as a dutiful son on the family farm, an Airman in the United States Air Force, an administrator in public school systems, or as I am currently, a citizen dedicated to civic and social change, I still feel like I am serving my country. As long as I have breath in my body, I will continue to serve. I am…still a soldier.

Legacy MVT: Having good conversational skills in your toolbox will help you keep your moral compass close at hand and always pointed true.

About the Author

LC Johnson lives with his wife, Gracie, and their little dog, Oscar, in Gwinnett County, Georgia. A resident of the newly established Peachtree Corners, Georgia, a town he helped guide into existence, LC and his wife, Gracie, enjoy a comfortable life with plenty to do, among people they truly like.

Their hometown is located in a county whose residents mirror the many faces LC has looked into all around the world during his tours of duty stretching over his sixty-plus years as a soldier in the military, educational system, and of social change throughout the world.

As an official Octogenarian, LC continues to serve on a number of influential boards throughout Georgia. He lives each day believing that we should all strive to do the most good by putting good conversational skills into our own personal toolboxes.

Made in the USA
Lexington, KY
29 May 2017